W9-DAU-483

DECISION MAKING
IN THE CHURCH

LUKE T. JOHNSON

DECISION MAKING
IN THE CHURCH

A Biblical Model

FORTRESS PRESS
PHILADELPHIA

Biblical quotations, unless otherwise noted, are from the Revised Standard Version of the Bible, copyright 1946, 1952, © 1971, 1973 by the Division of Christian Education of the National Council of the Churches of Christ in the U.S.A. and are used by permission.

COPYRIGHT © 1983 BY FORTRESS PRESS

All rights reserved. No part of this publication may be reproduced, stored in a retrieval system, or transmitted in any form or by any means, electronic, mechanical, photocopying, recording, or otherwise, without the prior permission of the copyright owner.

———————

Library of Congress Cataloging in Publication Data

Johnson, Luke Timothy.
   Decision making in the church.

    1. Bible. N.T. Acts X,1-XV,35—Criticism, interpretation, etc. 2. Decision-making, Group, in the Bible. 3. Decision-making, Group—Religious aspects—Christianity. I. Title.
   BS2625.2.J63 1983   262   82-17675
   ISBN 0-8006-1694-4

———————

9763H82   Printed in the United States of America   1-1694

For the students
at Yale Divinity School
who taught me

CONTENTS

Preface   9
Introduction   11
Chapter 1: Definitions   15

Decision Making in Groups   15
The Church as Community of Faith   23
Faith as the Obedient Hearing of God   25
Theology as the Articulation of Faith in the Church   28
Theology and the Narrative of Experience   31
The Normative Framework of the Scripture   33

Chapter 2: Difficulties   37

Some Scattered Witnesses   37
    1 Corinthians 5:1-5   40
    Matthew 18:15-20   41
    1 Corinthians 12-14   43
    Galatians 2:1-10   45

A Narrative Text: Acts 15:1-35   46
    The Use of Acts 15   48
    The Historical Difficulty   50
    The Literary Difficulty   53
    The Theological Difficulty   55

Chapter 3: Decisions   59

Divine Guidance and Human Decisions in Acts   59
Four Cases of the Church Making Decision   60
    The Election of Matthias (Acts 1:15-26)   60
    The Decision to Continue Preaching (Acts 4:23-31)   62

The Choosing of the Seven (Acts 6:1–6)   64
The Acceptance of Paul as a Disciple (Acts 9:26–30)   65

From Cornelius to the Council: Stages of a
  Church Decision   67
    The Conversion: The First Decision (Acts 10:1–48)   69
    Peter in Jerusalem: The Decision Defended
      (Acts 11:1–18)   74
    The Jerusalem Council: The Decision Opposed
      and Affirmed (Acts 14:26—15:35)   77

Decision Making as a Theological Process   86
Chapter 4: Discernment   89

Three Cases for Discernment   91
  The Leadership of Women in the Church   92
  Divorced and Remarried in the Church   93
  Homosexuality in the Church   95

Narrative and Discernment   97
Chapter 5: Devices   101

PREFACE

Once or twice in this book, I call it an "essay for idealists," and that is probably as good a description as any for this slender volume. It tries to place the decision-making process of the church within a biblical and theological framework. You may regard it as a curio, or as a Molotov cocktail. I can't make up my mind how to regard it. It is a book which seemed to force itself on me, and then develop a logic of its own. I certainly wrote it, but I am not altogether sure I like what I read in it. I don't know if this is because I did the job badly or well. If badly, I am embarrassed. If well, I am frightened.

They can't be blamed, of course, but others have had a part in the shaping of these ideas, if only because they listened and did not leave. Much of the material for chapters two and three was first prepared for the Luke-Acts task force of the Catholic Biblical Association in two papers: "The Use of Acts 15 in the Theology of the Church: A Scouting Report" (1978), and "The Church Reaching Decision: A Theological Reading of Acts 10–15" (1979). The constructive responses of Bill Kurz, Dennis Hamm, and Rea McDonnell were encouraging. In the summer of 1978 many of the ideas of chapter one were developed in three lectures given to the East Ohio Methodist Conference College of Preachers, under the rubric, "The Pastor as Theologian." David Wilcox enabled and abetted this venture, and can be praised or blamed as appropriate. A final group of victims were the participants in a Yale-Warner Memorial Presbyterian Church symposium held in Kensington, Maryland in 1982. David Graybill and Carol Strickland provided David Kelsey and me with an opportunity to talk through some of these ideas together. The benefit of Kelsey's conversation and writing to my own thought outweighs, I hope, any damage I may have done to his.

I owe most thanks to those Yale Divinity School students who shared so many narratives of faith with me over the past six years, who showed me that the ideas in chapter five can work if they are tried, and who cheered for Peter and Paul and James when they heard what they had done. At the close of a very enjoyable sojourn, this book is dedicated to them.

LUKE T. JOHNSON
New Haven, Connecticut
February 28, 1982

INTRODUCTION

Practical thinking is messy. Most of us are strong on theory, for theory is clear and clean and stands still. But thinking about the ever-shifting face of real life brings terror to the mind. The subject matter does not hold steady. Worse, it takes hold of the thinker, preventing distance and discretion. These qualities are admired before all others in science, so practical thinking is sometimes considered less serious than the sort given to molecules and mollusks. It is not, of course. It only requires quicker feet.

The subject of reaching decision in the church is such a practical topic in both the loose and strict sense. It is "useful" because it is something done by people in the church all the time; some thinking might be pertinent. It is also practical in the strict sense: it has to do, not with theory, but with practice (*praxis*). What the church does when it makes decisions concerns us here.

The subject matter is so common and deceptively available that it is necessary to back up a little and make clear what aspect of it demands attention and why. Otherwise, we might get lost. We might discover that some fundamental presupposition we thought we had shared suddenly divides us and keeps us from moving further. You might, for example, have something different in your mind when you say church than I do. Your understanding of "faith" and "theology" could be considerably removed from my own. We will begin, then, with some fundamental notions before moving on to the substance of this essay.

You can see that, however practical the goal of this book, it is going to involve some theory. This is not surprising. Practical issues have a way of cracking open the world of our presuppositions once we begin to ques-

11

tion them. You might also suspect that this is really an essay for idealists, and that is true, as well. This is not a sociological analysis, with
graphs and charts showing how dioceses and denominations reach decisions. The way groups act when they make decisions, however, is of
considerable interest to this discussion. Neither is this a strictly historical
study, although some documents from the past will demand more than
passing attention. And even though I do make some suggestions about
making decisions, this is not really a manual of instructions. I want to
think with you about the way decision making in the church can be a
theological process.

What you will find here, then, is a kind of theological reflection on the
nuts and bolts of the church's life. I have a bias. I think there ought to be
some connection between what a group claims to be, and the way it does
things. The church claims to be a community of faith. Is there any connection between this claim and its actual communal life? This could be
tested by looking at several places where churches express their life, but
a particularly important and revealing place is the process of reaching
decision.

I must admit to another bias, this one perhaps disproportionately important in my thinking on this issue. This bias says that when the church
makes decisions, the Bible ought somehow to be involved. This is a strong
but not terribly helpful bias, for it raises more problems than it settles. How
should the Bible be involved? Specters of proof-texting float before our
anxious eyes. If these shadows are to be dispersed, we must come to grips
with the legitimate and necessary connections between the use of Scripture in theology, the place of theology in the church, and the contribution
made by both to that process by which the church discerns and decides its
identity in the present for the future.

All of this means that a considerable space for backing up is necessary,
and that is what I want to do in the first chapter: back up far enough so
that the leap to the subsequent discussion is safe if not exhilarating. So that
we can understand each other as we go along, I want to begin by discuss-
ing some aspects of decision making by all groups: what does it involve?
What are the constitutive elements of group decision making, and how do
they interact? How might these apply to the church as a social group? After
these considerations, I will try to make clear my own understanding of the

church and theology, and the place of Scripture in both. If these preliminaries are made clear, then we may not in the end agree, but the basis for our disagreement will be easier to find.

1
DEFINITIONS

Our interest is in the process of reaching decision by the social group called the church. The fascinating but distracting issue of individual decision making must resolutely be left aside, except as it pertains to the life of the group. Whether decisions are actually ever made is something else we cannot prove but only assert. Talk about decisions implies that people are free to choose. Some philosophers deny that this happens. Since human freedom is illusory, they say, so also is the apparent freedom found in decisions. Choices can always be reduced to biological, psychological, and social forces. Neither the partial truth of this position nor its attractiveness need be denied. Much of the human enterprise is undoubtedly determined by the factors so minutely scrutinized by the detractors of freedom.

If the denial of determination is foolish, however, there is a hint of madness in the opinion which says choices are never free. The madness lies in the equation of reality with our ways of analyzing it. When we look at choices after the fact we can always find their causes. Hindsight reduces freedom to fate. Yet freedom is experienced in the act itself, even by those who deny it in their studies. In fact, the denial of freedom by one fated to that view is not worth much consideration. The notion of freedom appears to be, like the concept of God, necessary for its own effective rebuttal. So, I assume here that freedom is real and often a factor in the decisions made by individuals and groups. The forces of determination should also be given their due. Everything appearing to be free decision is not. Both congressional votes and political platitudes often have a certain admirable predictability.

Decision Making in Groups

Some group decisions are stimulated by the choices made by individual members of the group. Sometimes the group as such is required to act because of the frequency and vigor of individual actions threatening the group identity. Such is the case with deviance in behavior and heresy in doctrine. Groups have a fragile hold on their existence. They depend on the commitment of their members to the way things are done, and the reasons for so doing them. Groups have, therefore, only limited tolerance for diversity. When that tolerance is overstepped, the group will either dissolve or make decisions. Even apart from the challenges posed by the choices made by individuals, groups must make decisions for the body as a whole. No matter how small or large the group, whether it be family, club, school, city, state, or nation; as soon as the pronoun is "we" rather than "I," a group's decision-making mechanisms are invoked.

All groups make both *task decisions* and *identity decisions*. The distinction is a loose one, with disputed borders. *Task decisions* tend to raise identity issues, and *identity decisions* require expression by specific tasks. Still, the distinction has some validity. Task decisions concern the functions to be performed by the group, whether of the maintenance and upkeep variety ("How can we keep the machine going?"), or of the missions and vocation variety ("What does this machine make, anyway?").

When groups are virtually defined by a single *task*, they find that identity and task decisions are almost identical, and relatively easier to make. A group whose sole reason for existing is to explore caves would do well to have an expert spelunker at its head, and if it were transported to the Sahara Desert, would need to reconsider its future as a group. A "task force" appointed to study an economic problem has only that for its goal, and should care little about its members' lives apart from their expertise and ability to work together.

Identity decisions are also required of all groups. Membership questions fall into this category: who can be admitted to the group, and under what conditions? Decisions on boundaries also implicate the identity of the group: how can we define, symbolize, and keep effective the lines between "us" and "them"? A third type of identity question deals with discipline and correction within the group: how do we measure failure and success? How is one punished and the other rewarded? At what point can we no longer tolerate deviance? What does it mean when a member of the group is expelled? Decisions of this sort are made less on the basis of efficiency, as should be the case with task decisions, than on the basis of self-understanding. When decisions must be made concerning leadership and its right and responsibilities, task and identity questions both are involved.

The distinctions obviously oversimplify complex processes, but some groups tend to be defined more by the tasks they perform, while others by simply "being" a certain way. It is not always possible to distinguish one from the other since both kinds of groups make both task and identity decisions. Nevertheless, it is fair to say that groups defined by "being" a certain way (a "community of the pure," a "witness to the truth," a "school of the Lord's service") will find decisions concerning "identity" more difficult and threatening than those concerning tasks. For groups whose purpose is fulfilled by a certain kind of "doing," on the other hand, "task" decisions will be more critical.

In making decisions of any sort, a group *reveals* itself as a group, and it does this by *becoming itself* as a group. Decision making is a fundamental articulation of a group's life. The process by which decision is reached tells of the nature of the group in a way other forms of ritual sometimes miss. Perhaps a community loudly proclaims its democratic lifestyle— and at work, sleep, and meals, the members hold all things equally. But if the community's decisions are made by executive decree, the claim to equality is empty; the group actually has an authoritarian structure. If decisions on entrance and advancement, leadership and responsibility were made by a genuinely popular vote, that process would reveal the group to be democratic in a way that propaganda never could.

Qualifications for taking part in the decision-making process also tell us a great deal about the nature of the group. Property, gender, or age qualifications for voting give specific shading to the kind of democracy this is. The fact that we vote to make decisions tells us that we are a democracy. The fact that not all of us who are members of the group *can* vote tells us that this democracy is not absolute but relative. If it is possible for a member to *lose* a vote, that tells us how seriously we take responsibility or deviance. And if members of a group have the vote but do not *use* it, we learn of a profound alienation of the members from the life of the group.

The decision-making process in groups may be camouflaged, so that it takes effort to discover the genuine structure of the group. In complex social organisms, the obvious and hidden functions of structures frequently become mixed. In a large university, for example, the faculty may be convinced that it decides the direction of the school through its committees which debate and decide policy issues. But faculty meetings and committees often better serve the hidden functions of socialization and energy diffusion than the obvious function of governance. Meanwhile, a poorly legitimated but effective bureaucracy does the real steering. The fact that processes can be counterfeited and hard to detect, however, does not deny their power to reveal the group's nature when finally found. A university run by administrators rather than faculty may be an admirable society, but its decisions are likely to be made on the basis of financial or political considerations rather than strictly academic ones. To that extent, it may no longer be the kind of group its members still conceive it to be.

Groups, and the myths which legitimate them, are conservative by nature and resistant to change. It requires considerable energy for individuals simply to maintain, much less challenge, their social world. Many group decisions, as a result, tend to be made *implicitly*, following the path of least resistance. This is the path of "what we have always done." In the absence of challenge from without, the process of admission to the group, for example, will never change. Practice is reinforced by precedent. If only adult males have applied for membership in the past, then only adult males will have been admitted. The force of this precedent, however, will make the admission of anyone else a major adjustment. Along with the practice, the perceptions of the group become petrified. The continued admission of only adult males begins to suggest that this is a "males only" group. Structure reinforces ideology. If we are asked why we admit only males, we shall probably find reasons why ours is the sort of group in which only males *can* participate.

Practices become *explicit* in their structure and ideology when challenged by the possibility of change. It is only when adult women seek admission to our group that our previous habit and presuppositions will be called into question. The challenge to change forces a decision. Now the members must find reasons why women should or should not be admitted.

Let us suppose our mythical group is called "Scientists United." Now we must decide whether, in spite of our title, we have been all along simply a "male support group" (and can therefore legitimately exclude women), or have been a "scientific association" (which can find no reason for excluding women scientists). Whichever way the decision goes, the process of reaching it will show us the true identity of the group; the decision, furthermore, will give more definite shape to the group's identity than it had in earlier, innocent, and unchallenged times.

The threat of change forced groups to make its previously implicit choices explicit. In the process, it must identify both the challenge and its own nature as a group. The identification process is reciprocal. The challenge is perceived in terms of the group's previous understanding, but in turn, it calls to the surface aspects of that understanding which had been latent. Making decisions, then, always involves a process of *interpretation*. Even when carried out after the fact, such interpretation tries to get at the question, "Why did we do that?" and will likely answer it, "Because we are that kind of group." Once accustomed ways are called into question, both the voice of change and the voice of tradition require interpretation.

The demand for group interpretation raises other questions about the dynamics of decision making. Who in the group is responsible for carrying out this interpretation? Is the task entrusted to one person? If so, on what basis? Or are others involved in the interpretation? If so, how do they express their understanding? Do they interpret by their vote alone, or do they give voice to their understanding in any other way? And whose voices are listened to? Are those seeking membership, for example, included in the process? Are they interviewed to discover their reasons for seeking entrance? Or does such a hearing prejudice the issue by already inserting them into the decision-making process?

Other questions concern the *norms* by which the group interprets itself and makes decisions. The demand for decision challenges a group's identity and requires its interpretation. But where is the measure for this identity? Does our group have a constitution with by-laws? Do we operate on the basis of a collection of precedents? Do we find the measure for our identity in the body of stories and customs which forms our tradition? Do we have a "founding document" which we regard as authoritative?

Finding the normative expression of the group's identity only begins the interpretative process, for we must consider what role those norms will play when confronted by the pressure of the present situation and the current mood of the members. To state that the charter is normative does not yet say how it will be normative. Perhaps it does not appear to address the present circumstances at all, or only ambiguously. How much weight will be given to tradition and how much to the present, and who will do the weighing? The answers to these questions, too, tell us much about the nature of the group.

The dilemma of the group called "Scientists United" is simple enough to let me summarize the observations I have been making and suggestive enough to point toward the same process in the church. We remember that the group had only male members until women asked to join. Now what must we as a group do? First, we need to identify the challenge: are these sincere scientists seeking knowledge and collegiality, or are they women seeking only the disruption of male prerogatives? Second, we are pushed by that consideration to define more clearly our own identity: are we scientists who only happen to be male, or are we men who enjoy each other's company and only happen to dabble in science? Third, we need some normative expression of our identity which will help us determine it for the present, whether we find this in charter, constitution, or anecdotes. Fourth, the process of interpretation needs some coordination: who will give voice to the group's self-understanding, the president, secretary, best researcher, oldest member? Fifth, we must consider whose voices will be heard: are the women to be interviewed, or do we listen only to each other? Sixth, how will this whole process be ordered: do we meet as a committee of the whole, do we delegate it to a special subgroup, or do we hand it over to the president to decide, since we can't be bothered? Seventh, by what means will the decision be expressed: by vote, by executive decree, by inertia? In somewhat rough fashion, these questions describe the important elements of group decision making. Not all of them are always present, and certainly not always in equal proportion.

Some groups are shaped by more ultimate values and claim to serve more transcendent purposes than science clubs. The reinterpretation of their identity when challenged by change will be more intricate and far-reaching. For a club to admit women as fellow scientists is one thing (not altogether insignificant); but for a "Holy Remnant of the Lord" to admit "Sinners" to communion is quite another. Or, to make the obvious connection, for a male hierarchy to ordain women is similarly shocking. These sorts of decisions will be provoked only by the strongest stimulus and will require the most vigorous sort of interpretative process. For groups whose functions is to *be* a certain way in the world, decisions concerning membership, discipline, and expulsion are inevitably critical, and potentially dangerous to the stability of the group.

In a happy and logical world, one would expect some coherence to the process of decision making, and that the interpretation called forth by challenge would clearly reveal the self-understanding of a group. Explicit decisions ought to reveal the system of values by which a group lives and the framework within which implicit decisions had been made all along. If a large business corporation, for example, finds itself required to decide whether to continue or stop production of a product, we would expect that something of the business ethos would be revealed by the process of reaching that decision. The "symbolic world" of business understands above all that businesses exist to make profits. The challenge may be posed by a competitor's product cutting into the market. Perhaps this product's declining sales are affecting the market health of an entire line. In either case, the challenge will be interpreted consistently within the group's self-understanding as a profit-making enterprise. A secondary consideration, of course, may be the corporation's "image," how it is perceived by others, especially consumers and investors. It is important to be known as a bold yet trustworthy institution whose stability can be relied on. The juggling of products, therefore, and above all the impression of panic must be avoided. This consideration as well is directly tied to the profit motive.

The dynamics of decision making in large corporations are doubtless complex, but some factors will carry more weight than others. Whose voice will be heard? Cost-analysis figures and market projections will be studied like runes, but the testimony of assembly-line workers about the pleasure of packaging the product will not be heard. Those who sell the product will not have a voice. But the opinion of those who will buy the product is eagerly sought. The decision will finally be made by a small group of executives who may not even be known by the other members of the group, and whose function has nothing to do with the edification or education of those other members, but only the proper proportion of money flowing in and out.

Factors not considered are as significant as those which are. No corporation would attribute the decline in a product's popularity to the work of the Devil. Nor would a corporation (except in some unfortunate cases) try to discern "God's will" in its struggle to decide whether or not to continue production. These symbols and values are simply not part of the world-view of the corporation even at the implicit level. No challenge, therefore, can make them explicit. As for concern with the corporation's "image," it may be packaged in terms of folksy values, but seldom is there the attempt to genuinely maintain continuity with the expressed goals and values of the company's founders. Finally, there is no consideration given to whether or not the product is good for the buyer, in either the immediate or ultimate sense. This group does not exist to meet legitimate human needs; rather, the profit motive drives the group to create needs where none existed.

I do not suggest that there is something bad about this decision-making process in a large corporation. On the contrary, I find it refreshingly straightforward. The implicit values by which the corporation lives are given explicit expression in the making of a concrete decision. One may not like this symbolic world, but it is coherent. It may be more disturbing to find groups which claim to live by other values than these making decisions in a similar way.

My observations on the way groups go about reaching decision are too casual to claim sociological precision. But perhaps they are sufficiently accurate to be provocative and provide a framework for the rest of this discussion. Awareness of the factors at work in the decision-making process of all groups can make our appreciation of the church's practice keener and more realistic. If it is true that decision making is a process wherein a group's identity is revealed; if the challenge to change demands an interpretation in which the implicit self-understanding of the group is made explicit; if this interpretation requires a fresh reading of the group's normative charter; if the voices which are allowed to speak and the voice which speaks most decisively show the structure of the group; then, what do we learn about the nature of the church as we see it reaching decision? Is its proclaimed nature revealed? Is its essential self-understanding given articulation? Or is there a disparity between what the church claims to be and what its way of deciding the future shows it to be?

The answer to these questions will not be found in this book. They can be answered, in fact, only in each of those places where the church is to be found making decisions. I am writing an essay for idealists, after all, and must be more concerned with the ''ought'' than with the ''is.'' Before I am able to proceed with even that implausible task, however, I must consider some of the fundamental notions which will run throughout the essay. What do I mean by church, and where do I think it is found? What is the symbolic world of the church, implicit in all its choices but made explicit by challenge? What is the measure of the church's self-understanding? How is this understanding mediated within the group? These are questions large and unwieldy enough to fill volumes of systematic theology. In the remarks which follow, therefore, you will not find a cautious, even-handed discussion, but a series of idiosyncratic opinions. The opinions, moreover, have been shaped to a considerable degree by the reading of the New Testament, to which I will shortly invite you. This exercise contains an inevitable, but I hope not vicious, circularity.

The Church as Community of Faith

It is as hard to find a workable notion of the church as social group as it is to figure out the boundaries of a multinational conglomerate. "Church" is a term applied to many kinds of groups, ranging from the smallest gathering of two or three—"in my name"—at the local level, through a wide variety of sects and denominations, spiraling into ever more complex associations and alliances, all the way to some cosmic understanding of church as "catholic" or "ecumenical," or even in the broadest possible sense, "all those who call on the name of the Lord." The question "where is the church?" not only raises theological hackles but also defies sociological determination.

The competing claims and counterclaims of sects and denominations must be weighed, of course, but we must also look hard to distinguish in each case formal legal structure from a living social group. All groups have structure. As soon as two or three meet more than once and spend any time together, they will, no matter how "equal," begin to develop a sense of order and leadership. Even the most charismatic assembly involves something of "institution." That said, it is not only possible but necessary to distinguish between relative degrees of "life" and "order" in the vast continuum which runs from store-front church to the World Council of Churches. And the more organizational complexity we meet, the more we sense the power of "order" over that of "life." The question "where is the church?" cannot be answered in terms either of organizational charts or ecumenical conferences. It must be answered by another question: "Where does the church really live?" The church in the strict sense is found where there is a specific group of people who assemble together to call on the name of the Lord in prayer and fellowship.

However much our reflexes have been conditioned to do so, it is a mistake to think of the church first of all in terms of a worldwide organization or alliance of organizations. The decision-making process there at the ecumenical or world council level is far removed from the living pulse of

God's people. The level of international and interdenominational conversation is important, and must be considered. It should be considered, however, in the last place, not in the first.

The church in its first and living sense means the local assembly, God's convocation in a particular time and place. The doctrine of the church must begin at this local level. So, therefore, should the study of how the church makes decisions. Why? Because it is only at the local level that we can legitimately speak of a "community" at all. Where there is no possibility for face-to-face interaction among the members of a community, then it has ceased to be a community. It has begun to change from organism to organization. The promise of Jesus was to be where two or three were gathered in his name (Matt. 18:20). Certainly, there can be more than two or three. But the promise implies that there can be a physical "gathering." Beyond a certain number, such "gathering" becomes difficult. If the church does not live first at this local level, it does not live at all.

Looked at in this way, the church can be recognized as an intentional community. People belong to the church because they choose to belong. The church may practice infant baptism, or even speak of being "born into" the faith. But the community exists in active form because of the present conscious commitment of its members. All churches distinguish between "membership rolls" and "active members," and the distinction is just. It points to the dividing line between legal entity and the living organism. The church's own symbolic understanding, of course, qualifies this identification as an intentional community by claiming it is called into existence by God. Even as a response to God, however, the choice of individual members makes the church exist at any given moment.

As in other communities constituted by choice, the church has a set of symbols which its members share with varying degrees of awareness and commitment. This symbolic world is sometimes simply called "faith," and those who belong to the community are called "believers" or "the faithful." A shorthand for the complex system of creeds and convictions which expresses the church's symbolic world is "the faith." Thus the church can fairly be called a community of faith.

There are different views even within the church concerning the exclusiveness of this communal set of symbols. Some say that this thing called "faith" is found only within the boundaries of the visible community. Others claim that it is found wherever people seek God, even if they cannot share the worship and fellowship of other believers. Still others (and I) hold that genuine faith is found at least implicitly outside the visible church. Indeed, a fundamental function of the church as social group is to make explicit in the world what is implied by the stirrings of hearts everywhere for ultimate truth, and therefore for the true God. If faith, furthermore, can be found outside this group, so also within the group faith is found in the most diverse forms and degrees of health. "Faith" does not describe the finished response of all in the group so much as the norm for those responses, which always fall short of the one for whom they reach.

If we identify the church as a community of faith, the process of decision making ought to make the structures and implications of this response to reality called "faith" more explicit. *Reaching decision in the church should be an articulation of faith.* To see how this might be so, we need to look more closely at this term which is central to the church's identity.

Faith as the Obedient Hearing of God

Just as it is important to locate and identify the church as a living organism, so is it helpful to begin with the primary meaning of "faith" from which other meanings derive. Like the term "church," it can have several meanings or senses. It can refer to the whole symbolic universe of the Christian tradition. More narrowly, it can mean the "structure of belief" succinctly summarized in creeds and confessions. "Faith" is also used to describe personal commitment. This use has two distinct emphases. One way of understanding the commitment is in terms of intellectual conviction. Faith is seen as the assent of the mind (and heart) to revealed truths. This is a legitimate and important understanding of faith, but it is still secondary and derivative.

Faith in its proper and active sense describes the response of one person to another in trust and obedience. It is a deeply responsive hearing of another's word, or call. Theological faith is the response by a human being to the call of God, that is, the Word of God as it is revealed in the fabric of worldly existence. The opposite of such theological faith is idolatry. Idolatry is a way of responding to existence which says that the world we see is all there is. Idolatry flees the terror of contingency and attempts to seize hold of life as a possession. Faith is the response to existence which says that the one who is not seen is most real, and that although contingent, we are established in being every moment by the power of God. At every moment, God calls us beyond our partial life and perceptions to the experience and knowledge of himself. Faith is that directing of human freedom which says "yes" both to God and to the human condition. In so doing, it recognizes that part of the human condition, never fully overcome, is the desire to rest in what we can claim as our own. It recognizes as well that the call of God is to a freedom which is frightening in its capacity to possess us but not to be possessed by us.

In the response called faith, the human person asserts that God is not only "real," but that God is what is most real. God is not a vague idea, left over when everything is counted, but is active and alive, and intrudes into human existence—into my existence—not only in the past but also in the present; not only gently but sometimes with rude force; not only in experienced presence but also in experienced absence; not alone in good but also in evil. God creates the world and all that is in it, from nothing, every minute, so that the world and all its peoples might, above the abyss, trust the hand which holds and obey the voice which calls us, and sing, "You are the maker, and to you belongs the glory!"

Because God intrudes into the comfortable space we cling to for self-definition and calls us out to a wider truth, divine revelation continues in our world. God acts now. And since God's activity is meaningful, the Word of God is continually spoken and requires hearing. Faith says that God did not stop speaking when the Prophets died, nor even when God's Word was enfleshed in Jesus Christ. Faith asserts that God's Word is enunciated in every age and in every human life by the work of God's Holy Spirit.

At the same time, faith cannot pretend that God's Word is clear and easily available to human understanding. Because it is the Word of the one who moves beyond human grasp and avoids human naming, and because it is a Word spoken in and through the circumstances of worldly life, it is ambiguous and requires cautious and humble deciphering. The first interpretation takes place in the response of faith itself. The obedience of faith demands the scrutiny of God's Word here and now. What in this context is the legitimate human project, and what the project of God which calls all others into account? In few cases is such scrutiny easy; in some it seems nearly impossible. In the powerful disturbance of our complacency, we may recognize the Holy, but that does not yet yield knowledge of the call it makes to us.

Since God calls us anew every moment, the response of faith is never-ending. This hearing demands an asceticism of attentiveness. There is never a moment before death when faith can say, "Enough, it is finished," for the Word of God to each individual is not fully spoken until that death. God's Word unfolds with every breath we breathe. Faith moves constantly from death to life: death to our prior understanding, footholds and securities; and life, given freely each moment by another. A perilous progress. For this reason, we can recognize Jesus as the pioneer and perfector of our faith. He moved in obedience to the death of the cross, and when he wished to live on his own terms, he said "yes" to the one who called him.

Where the church exists as something more than institution or ethical society, it is marked by this kind of faith. The church is a paschal community, dying in order to live. In the lives of its individual members, faith seeks to discern the call of God in their particular circumstances. As a group, the community as well seeks to discern the Word spoken to this people in the challenges of the present moment. The identity of the church is always being shaped by its response to God's call in the context of its worldly life.

The relevance of this for our present discussion should be clear: the *implicit* choices of the group, which the challenge to change ought to make explicit, are the choices of faith for God's Word. This means, in turn, that the process of making decisions in the church will involve the interpretation of God's Word. The church is called into existence in the first place, sustained and addressed by the activity of God both within it and outside it. The church believes, therefore, that—however darkly—it is being called as a group by the working of God in its members. This working of God requires scrutiny, discernment. Is this truly God's Word which is being spoken to us in these circumstances, or a counterfeit of that Word? Discernment, the process of sorting, evaluating, and distinguishing among competing voices, is already a kind of decision.

God's Word in another sense requires discernment by the church. There is no possibility of recognizing the action of God in the present as *God's* action, unless we have some knowledge of God's work in the past. The Word of God in Scripture, therefore, is an essential aspect of the church's discernment in decision making. It is in that Word—that set of symbols and stories—that the church finds the grammar for deciphering the Word spoken here and now. The observation leads us to the role of theology in the life of the church, which is the life of faith.

Theology as the Articulation of Faith in the Church

Faith is not first of all attachment to a body of doctrines but a process of responding in obedience and trust to God's Word. God has given us the possibility of hearing the Word, since it was spoken in the humanity of Jesus, which we share, and since it continues to be spoken by the Holy Spirit, which dwells in us. So also theology is not first of all the study of doctrines, but a process of reflection on this response of faith. The classic definition of theology, "faith seeking understanding" (*fides quaerens intellectus*), remains always valid. Faith seeks to understand the one to whom it responds. It also, thereby, seeks to understand itself, and the implications of being so called and so gifted to respond.

Theology is an articulation of faith in at least three ways. First, theology articulates faith in the sense of "giving voice" to faith. Part of theology's task is tending the story of faith and keeping alive the possibility of its continuing. Second, theology articulates faith by showing its structure: how do the various aspects of this living response fit together? Third, theology articulates faith by searching out the connections between this most fundamental and pervasive response to reality, and all the other responses life demands. If we say "yes" to God, what does this imply for saying "yes" to the human condition and "yes" to the world?

The faith which seeks understanding is not just that of an individual alone; it is the faith of the *church*. This statement can be understood in two ways. Conventionally, the "faith of the church" designates precisely the creeds, doctrines, and traditions which the theologian would study. But if we understand the faith of the church in dynamic terms, then the search of theology for understanding involves the active discernment of the responses to God being made by individuals as they together, as church, seek to decide in favor of God.

Who is qualified for this? It is not a task only of appointed or even of gifted individuals within the assembly. The theological task is implied by the very life of faith itself. Every Christian is called to do theology in this sense. Every Christian must seek an understanding of his or her response to God and the implications of that response for the rest of life. Everyone in the church must exercise discernment concerning the response of the church as a whole to the challenge of God's Word. The church itself is the locus of theology. It is not just where the theologian works; theology is, rather, a church task. Because everyone in the church is required to interpret his or her life before God, everyone in this community is also required to do theology. Everything else we mean by theology derives from this fundamental sense. Otherwise, the "faith" which seeks understanding is removed from the pulse of human life, and therefore of God's revelation in the world.

That everyone in the church is called to do theology in this way does not mean that some people in the community do not exercise this ministry in a special way. A look at other articulations of the church's life helps us realize how ministries make explicit for the group what is implicit in the lives of all. In worship, the leader gives voice and gesture to the adoration in the hearts of all. If only the leader prays, there is no community worship, but only private piety performed in public. Likewise in works of mercy, those who reach out to the needy in the church's name make explicit the openhandedness implicit in the lives of its members; otherwise, the symbolization of the community's faith is counterfeit. So with theology: all Christians are required to interpret their lives before God, but some in the church have the ability to make these diverse interpretations available to all, and of articulating in a more formal fashion the implications of the choices being made by all the members.

Above all, the theologian helps the church to form and understand its response *as* a group, helps it pull together the many individual interpretations of God's Word into a community discernment which prepares for decision. The theologian may be preacher or teacher, may be ordained or not, may be now one person, now another. But the theologian's interpretation of how God is calling us as a group will be alive and pertinent only if the same process of interpretation is going on in the lives of individual believers within the community. The case is the same as with worship and work: without the implicit process, the explicit gesture is meaningless. But here, the situation is even more acute.

If the people are not themselves seeking to determine the Word of God in the tangle of their individual and shared lives, how can they *discern* the accuracy and adequacy of the theologian's interpretation of that Word for the group? The church, as a group, as a gathering of believers, must test the Spirit's movement. This means to test the word of interpretation spoken in the assembly concerning the movement of the Spirit. If only one is interpreting, then the process fails. In that atmosphere, both false prophecy and demagoguery flourish. This also means that a theologian who is not in contact with the faith-life of an actual church runs the danger of having nothing to say, and becoming a theologian only in name. The discernment of the ''practical life'' of the Christian community *is* the cutting edge of theology. The more intellectually elaborate studies of doctrinal and systematic theology depend on a healthy pastoral theology for their life.

When theology is understood as a process of interpreting God's Word within the believing community, the unending nature of its task becomes clear. Theology needs to be renewed in every age, for the call of faith is always new. The subject matter of theology is not only the record of how God acted in the past, but above all how God is acting in the present. Furthermore, the call of God comes to us in the structures of worldly life, which themselves are constantly in flux. The implications of the faith response, therefore, cannot be fixed absolutely, but require an ever-renewed discernment by the community of faith. We change, and the structures of our world change; but more than that, the God who calls us is alive and moves ahead of us at every moment. Theology is always a catch-up ball game. As the obedience of faith demands a constant alertness to the movement of God's Spirit in the life of an individual, so does theology call for constant *attentiveness* to the work of the Spirit in the church's life here and now.

The theologian, then, is one within the church who articulates for all what has first been experienced by everyone who believes. By such articulation, the theologian *reminds* the community of its own deepest convictions, which are always in danger of being lost in the welter of worldly life. The theologian can remind the church of them only if they are alive for the theologian as well: first, God is alive and active in the world. Second, God here and now intrudes into human existence in powerful, sometimes frightening, and frequently ambiguous ways. Third, this intrusion presents the call of God to obedience and trust. Fourth, as the call is never-ending, so is the obedience of faith never finished, so that the church can never say, "enough." Fifth, the possibility of our identifying the work of God in the circumstances of moment depends on our knowledge and understanding of God's activity in the past. Sixth, the possibility for this recognition is given by the symbols and stories of the Bible. This last point suggests another way of describing the function of theology within the life of faith.

Theology and the Narrative of Experience

One of the ways the theologian serves the church is by helping it to tell its story. If we only appreciate storytelling as a pleasant diversion, we will not grasp the importance of this function. The study of societies—primitive and complex alike—shows us that although some forms of storytelling do serve a recreational purpose, others perform a more fundamental, *re-creational* role within the life of communities, shaping both the group and its understanding of reality. This kind of storytelling has to do with personal and group identity. The story of my life—if I can tell it—reveals who I am. Our communal story—if we can give it shape—tells others, and first of all ourselves, how we have come to be who we are. In the life of groups we find such storytelling in the myths of origin and those which accompany rites of passage. In the life of individuals, such personal storytelling is found in confession or therapy, where the telling of the story whole not only expresses a stage of intimacy and trust but also reveals at once to the other and to the self who one is.

Such personal and revelatory storytelling is an ordered form of personal or group memory, and memory *is* identity. Amnesia is a terrible affliction precisely because the loss of the past means the loss of the present as well. If I cannot remember who I have been, then I do not know who I now am. The same is true for groups: forgetting our past means ignorance of our present and the forfeiture of our future. It is here we find the critical importance of tradition for the life of groups. The real business of tradition is not the securing of the past, but the ensuring of a future. Only when we know how the story has run to this point can we responsibly decide how the plot might now develop. Humans are creatures who make up their stories as they go along. In them, they find both their identity and meaning. But it is not a random process. The story can only move forward as story, that is, with meaning, when it appropriates the past. Otherwise, there is not really change. Where there is no continuity, there is only meaningless movement.

Personal storytelling inevitably involves selection and shaping. Because we are telling the story of our experience—trying to order our memory of ourselves as we have existed in the world—and because our experience continues, we are constantly revising our story. Our past looks different to us at every moment. Our present experience influences our *selection* as to what out of the past we remember as significant. Because I am having a miserable day, I remember that ''my mother told me I'd have days like this.'' The pressure of the present makes various points of the past pertinent. The same force causes us to *shape* that memory of the past into forms usable in the present. My mother probably never said in so many words, ''You'll have days like that,'' but from all her care and counsel in the past, I shape my memory of her into this more universal and pithy shape. We make up our stories as we go along, and it is always a revisionist history. As with individuals, so with groups.

Experience and interpretation affect each other in this kind of story-telling. My story as I know it up to now—the way I understand myself in the world—gives me the categories for perceiving my present experience. No matter how powerful or profound, no experience is utterly naked. Already in the very act of sensation, we are interpreting on the basis of our past perceptions. We ''see'' the grass growing, and not the earth receding, because that is the way our story runs. We extend our hand to another for shaking, rather than reach for a weapon or flee, because our story causes us to see the outstretched hand of the other as a friendly gesture. When the handshake *is* friendly, my perceptions get reinforced, and my story requires no rereading.

But the effect of experience on interpretation can take another form. Experiences can be so radical or powerful or surprising that they not only stretch, but snap our categories of perception. If the other person grabs my hand and claps it into a handcuff, or if he cuts my hand, I must reconsider the place of handshakes in my story. So every challenge to change forces us to reread our story with new eyes.

Of all the stories humans can tell, the most fundamental one is surely their religious history, the story of their experience of God in the world. Strangely, however, this story is seldom told by individuals in the faith assembly. And when it is, it is unfortunately done in a manner which shows little reflective understanding. Yet, if God is alive and active at every moment, and if people are being called to faith by God's activity, then there must be such a story, at least implicitly, in the lives of all those who believe. Why is it not being told? And why do those who overcome embarrassment and try to speak this story find that they do not even have the words to tell it? We will look more closely at these questions in the last chapter of this book.

For now, I simply state my conviction that one of the tasks of theology is to help the church both hear and then tell its story. Therefore, the theologian needs to interpret both parts of the story: that which has already been told and that which is being spoken. The theologian seeks to make explicit the shape of God's Word being spoken to the church in the present circumstances, and how the church's decisions might continue the story of God's people. To do this, the theologian must listen to the narratives of those who believe—including the theologian's *own* story. The theologian also needs to interpret the story which has gone before: how has God worked among the people in the past? By what means can we recognize, if not God's face, then the trail of God's mercy and justice as they grace and frighten us? Without the means of perception given us by the story of our past history with God, we shall not be able to discern God's Word being spoken now. Without knowing of the Holy Spirit, its fruits, and its transforming power, how can we perceive the Spirit creating and sanctifying among us now?

We should make no mistake: the experience of God or the experience of God's absence is not accessible for casual perusal. It requires careful attention and delicate diagnosis. The process of discernment is risk-filled and never self-validating. The interpretation of the present moment is perilous, prone to error, always in need of renewal and revision. But such interpretation is the absolutely fundamental and necessary task of theology in the church. Without it, there is no subject matter.

The Normative Framework of the Scripture

The first part of the story is equally difficult to interpret. Not only is our shared Christian story a long one, but it is varied, fragmented, and filled with conflict and contradiction. Parts of it are lost in darkness, parts of it distorted by sin and neglect. There is everywhere shadow. The theologian therefore looks to some part of the story that can stand as normative for the rest, that is, which can give a frame for the proper understanding of the story which precedes us, and for the story which unfolds as we tell it. The theologian and other believers claim to find this normative framework in the canon of the Scripture, the Old and New Testaments.

The theologian seeks there the interpretative tools for discerning the story of the present. The decision to regard the canon of the Old and New Testaments as normative—as providing a sort of measure for authentic life before God—does not result from scientific inquiry, nor from historical research. The decision to regard these historically conditioned documents as having a normative force for every age of the church is a decision of faith. It is preeminently a church *decision*. In fact, it is one of the decisions which constitutes the church as such in every generation. The canon and the church are correlative in this sense: without the community regarding them as addressing it in an authoritative and normative way, these ancient writings would not be Scripture. On the other hand, without such a fixed frame of understanding, which mediates the identity of the community from age to age, there would not exist any historical community identifiable as the church in the first place. It is an expression of the church's faith to regard these writings as prophetic for every age, and therefore speaking God's Word. Canonization, therefore, is more than the residue of past decisions. It is a decision renewed by the church every time it reads these writings in the assembly for worship; when it looks to these writings alone as its unmeasured measure of self-understanding; when it allows these writings to question and interpret its present existence in a way it will let no other writings do.

As one who articulates the faith of the church, the theologian asserts this authoritative function of the Scripture in the life of the community, and in the reaching of decisions. It is not the theologian's role to decide *how* texts are to be normative. The theologian serves the church by allowing the text from the past and the text of the present to enter mutual interpretation. The theologian thereby helps provide the context for the discernment of God's Word now by allowing that Word to be shaped and questioned by God's Word in the Scripture. When that Word is brought into conversation with the present, it also becomes reread and reinterpreted because of God's continuing revelation in the stories of the people. The theologian does not interpret the Scripture alone, any more than the theologian interprets the moment alone. The church discerns and decides on behalf of God. The theologian helps this happen by allowing the Scripture to speak to life, and the word of life to speak to the Scripture, and this within the assembly of God's people.

These comments presuppose the availability of the writings in the Old and New Testaments for theological reflection within the assembly. To say that the Old and New Testaments provide the symbols and stories necessary for the discernment of God's Word in the stories of people today, implies both the pertinence of these writings to life and the perception of that pertinence by the people. Neither the presupposition nor implication may be valid for many churches or even for many theologians today. It is to that problem we now turn: how can the Scripture be made available for the church seeking to reach decision, and thereby express its identity as a community of faith?

I will not even try to answer the question in general, for I do not think there is a general answer. Rather the question can only be answered for particular writings in particular situations. Attempts at making the Scripture relevant for contemporary readers—the art of hermeneutics—usually have to do with the private reading of the texts by individuals. But the Scripture is first of all a church collection. These texts were written to be read before many hearers at worship, and so they are read in the church today. They are also read for purposes of public discussion and discernment. The Scripture as Scripture is appropriated by a community. Therefore, the act of interpretation (the hermeneutical process) must also involve the community. Another tendency of hermeneutics has been to search for one way of making the texts relevant. It has sought a mode of mediating the texts of Scripture by some rational construct or other. As a result, those texts which do not fit the construct do not get read, and are called ''irrelevant.'' But there can be no one way of mediating texts so diverse to an audience so diverse as the church. The writings were written at different times and places for differing purposes. And they speak through different literary forms. Theological interpretation in the church, therefore, must take seriously the diversity of the writings in the canon, and the diversity of the church not only in every age, but even in every locale in the same age. The relevance of texts will be proven, not by philosophical or rhetorical analysis, but by the use of them in the churches. The first theological task is to allow the conversation to start. How the parts of the story will connect depends on the discernment and decision of particular communities in specific places.

For the conversation to begin, however, there must be more than one voice, and it is to the problem regarding the Word of God in Scripture I now turn. I have two questions in mind. First, is there any hope of finding in the Scripture a symbolic expression or story which can help us determine the adequacy of our own dynamics of decision making in the church? If so, where, and in what fashion? Second, can our way of going about this interpretation in the specific case of decision making suggest ways in which the scriptural witness might be appropriated by the theology of the church in other cases and with other texts? Our starting point will be with the problems facing the venture.

2

DIFFICULTIES

We are looking for scriptural passages which can address the church's ways of reaching decision as a group. We need passages speaking of the church as a group, not just as individuals within the group, and speaking of decision making as a human process, not simply as a reported event, or one caused only by God. These criteria narrow our search to the New Testament, for the obvious reason that the church as such is not found in the Old Testament. For our discussion, the New Testament witnesses address the church's practice and self-understanding more directly.

Even within the New Testament, there are not many useful texts. Fewer still are extensive. Most of the passages about decision making are fragmentary, in the sense that they come at the issue only partially or indirectly. A group of narrative texts, on the other hand, rather fully display the decision-making process. The fragmentary texts, because they are in the form of exhortations and directives, are more easily regarded as theologically pertinent. The narratives do not appear to yield any norms.

Two separate interpretative difficulties face the reader from the beginning. The first concerns the relative importance to be given to the witnesses. Indiscriminate harmonizing is always bad method. In this case, however, there is something to be said for viewing the fragmentary texts as complementing the fuller ones, so long as this procedure does not detract from their own distinctive voice. I will first survey these partial and scattered references, to see how they might fit within a more complete picture. But then, a second and more difficult question needs to be faced: how can narrative passages be freed to become vehicles for theological reflection?

Some Scattered Witnesses

The place one would most like to find texts concerning decision making is the letters of Paul, and this for two reasons. First, Paul's focus is always fixed on the life of the local assembly. Apart from Ephesians, Paul refers to *church* as the people called together by God in a particular locality. Second, Paul always seeks to delineate the theological implications of the church's common activity.

Unfortunately, there is relatively little in Paul directly usable. What there is enriches the picture yet to be developed by the narratives. Although Paul constantly issues apostolic instructions and exhortations, demanding decisions of his communities, his letters rarely show us how the community might go about reaching those decisions. This lack might be attributed to Paul's claim of personal apostolic authority over his churches and his extraordinary involvement in their life. But since the other New Testament epistolary literature contains even less information than Paul on this subject, it may only be that procedures for reaching decision were sufficiently practiced and understood to require little underscoring.

Paul's letters contain some instructions concerning actions and attitudes relevant to the process of reaching decision in the church. In 1 Tim. 5:1–21, for example, Paul not only directs his delegate on the proper attitude he should have toward diverse members of the church (5:1–2) and sets guidelines for the treatment of widows (5:3–16), but demands that certain procedures be followed when local leaders are accused of wrongdoing by others in the community. He insists that no charge be admitted except on the evidence of two or three witnesses (5:19). This practice not only recalls the norm set in Deut. 19:15—an example of using the Scripture to validate the church's practice—but it also shows us the involvement of more than the interested parties in a dispute which affects the well-being of the group as a whole. Paul insists above all that prejudice and partiality are to be avoided in settling such complaints (5:21). Apart from the presence of the witnesses, however, we do not see the assembly as such involved here. It is Paul's delegate who is to carry out these instructions.

It is characteristic of Paul, in fact, to stress individual responsibility for making decisions. In his treatment of the unrest caused by different observances in the Church of Rome, Paul insists that all will have to answer to God for their own way of life (Rom. 14:4,12), and rejects any notion that individuals within the church can judge the life of others (14:4,10). He desires the mutual acceptance of legitimate differences within the church (14:13–14; 15:7). Each person must discern and decide what is best for him or herself (14:5). At the same time, however, each person also has the responsibility of acting in a way which builds up the community in faith

(14:19; cf. also Phil. 2:4). The approach is virtually identical in his discussion of eating meat offered to idols in the first letter to the Corinthians (1 Corinthians 8–10). Again he emphasizes the obligation to obey one's own conscience in such matters (1 Cor. 10:27–29), and the need for mutual edification (1 Cor. 8:12–13); but he does not suggest that the general issue, "Should Corinthian Christians eat meat offered to idols?" be decided by that church as a whole.

Paul's emphasis on individual discernment and decision is derived from his conviction concerning the spiritual nature of the Christian group. Not only charismatic leaders, but all believers have received the Holy Spirit (1 Cor. 12:13). Because of this, all in the community have been called to freedom (Gal. 5:13) and enjoy the freedom of God's children (Gal. 4:1–7) who have been released from fear (Rom. 8:14–17). The Spirit provides the power for a new way of existence. It is also the power which enables Christians to interpret that existence (1 Cor. 2:12), and make choices consistent with it. So Paul tells the Galatians, "If we live by the Spirit, let us also walk by the Spirit" (Gal. 5:25). Each Christian, therefore, is capable, and therefore required, to interpret his or her life before God in the concrete choices demanded by worldly existence.

Paul by no means suggests that this is an automatic or easy process. But the transforming power of the Spirit enables people to "prove [or 'test'] what is the will of God, what is good and acceptable and perfect" (Rom. 12:2). The testing process, moreover, is not entirely individualistic. It is true that Paul can say in Gal. 6:4, "Let each one test his own work," but he prepares for that statement by one coming just before it, "If a man is overtaken in any trespass, you who are spiritual should restore him in a spirit of gentleness" (Gal. 6:1; cf. also Col. 3:13). The exhortation implies some degree of communal discernment and correction, like that found in the command of James 5:19–22.

The church's responsibility for discerning the diverse movements of the Spirit within it is stated directly in 1 Thess. 5:19–22: "Do not quench the Spirit, do not despise prophesying, but test everything; hold fast what is good, abstain from every form of evil." These are plural imperatives in the Greek. The testing process is one required of the church as a group. This passage has some similarity to one outside the Pauline writings. In 1 John 4:1, we read, "Test the spirits to see whether they are of God; for many false prophets have gone out into the world." This passage deals with the problem of sorting out competing claims to spiritual authority and leadership. In Paul, the testing is done on the sort of behavior the Spirit appears to motivate, especially in prophecy. In both passages, the community as such is told to test, but in neither case is it told how to test.

These references are scattered, but cumulatively they point to the realization that, even in a spiritual community, the impulses of the Spirit are not always obvious and may even be counterfeited. There is need for constant discernment. We have nowhere seen any indication that the church should judge an individual member. The emphasis, rather, has been on the judgment each must face before God. The discernment demanded of individuals, however, clearly takes place in a spiritual community which, as a group of people, bears some responsibility for the articulation of the Spirit's life within it, for it has been told, "Test every spirit."

1 Corinthians 5:15

When the discernment process is not being carried out by individuals, their choices can threaten to falsify the community's identity. The members may claim to live by the Spirit, but their actions may betray the Spirit's nature. When this happens, it becomes necessary for the church to exercise a more drastic sort of group discernment, if it is to retain its own integrity. We find an example in 1 Cor. 5:1–5. The passage is short but raises a number of problems. Whatever the precise nature of the man's offense it is clear that this member of the Corinthian congregation had overstepped the bounds of acceptable diversity and had fallen into dangerous deviance. Here it is not a question of legitimate freedom possibly causing offense, as with eating meat offered to idols. When a Christian behaves openly in the church in a manner offensive even to pagans (1 Cor. 5:1), with no objection being made, the identity of the church as a people set apart by God for sanctification (1:2) is called into question. The boundary between "the saints" and "the world" (5:9–10) has collapsed, and the church has lost its reason for existing. The body no longer symbolizes the spirit. The situation in Corinth is exacerbated by the arrogance of the community (5:2) which leads it to judge between its teachers (1:12; 3:4) but not attend to the sort of discernment required if it is to remain God's church.

Paul insists that the community recognize and reaffirm its true identity. It must come together as the church to deal with this issue (5:4–5). Paul by no means leaves the decision up to them, however. Perhaps he thinks they had shown little capacity to use discernment. Instead, as one who is their father (4:15), an apostle (9:1) who certifiably has the Spirit of God

(7:40), he directs them to hand over the offender to Satan (5:5). This is a ritual of some obscurity, but is clearly a form of excommunication. When the community gathers, it is in the name of the Lord Jesus, and although Paul is absent in body, he is present with them in spirit at the assembly (5:3). The excommunication is intended to work for the man's ultimate salvation (5:5). For the community, however, this ritual exclusion serves the purpose of reasserting its identity as the temple of God where the Spirit dwells (3:16), and therefore as a cleansing (cf. 5:6–7).

Paul supports the excommunication by appeal to Scripture: ''Drive out the wicked person from among you,'' (Deut. 17:7), and Paul cites it from the Greek translation (the *Septuagint* = LXX) in 1 Cor. 5:13. Because this Christian community continues the story of God's people, earlier parts of the story provide norms for its own communal life (cf. also 1 Cor. 10:1–11; Rom. 15:4). Paul does not use the Deuteronomy passage mechanically. It dealt with the evil of idolatry among the people Israel, and advocated the death of the offender. By applying this passage to a sexual offense, which was to be punished by excommunication, Paul extends the meaning of the earlier passage. By so doing, of course, he also reinterprets it.

The extreme case of excommunication shows how Paul saw the need for the church to exercise discernment concerning its own life: ''Is it not those inside the church whom you are to judge?'' (1 Cor. 5:12). Only because the Corinthian Church failed in this decision-making process has Paul stepped in from outside to save and chasten the community, and to reassert his legitimate authority over it. It is not certain that we find another reference to this excommunication in 2 Cor. 2:5–11, but it is likely. Paul refers to a ''punishment by the majority'' which was carried out (2 Cor. 2:6), and which he had insisted on to test them and see if they were obedient (2:9). And, as in 1 Cor. 5:5, Satan is viewed as standing just outside the Church's boundaries (2 Cor. 2:11). Paul recommends that the one punished now be forgiven, comforted, and regarded with love (2:7–8). The church which exercises discipline as a group is also capable of forgiving and restoring to communion as a group. The attitude Paul here recommends corresponds to that found in Gal. 6:1 and Col. 3:13.

Matthew 18:15-20

The problem of discipline and excommunication is also addressed in Matt. 18:15–20. The passage appears to prescribe disciplinary practice for a particular community. Two of Matthew's three uses of the term "church" (*ekklēsia*) occur in this short passage (Matt. 18:17; cf. also 16:18). Here it is not a case of deviant behavior threatening the spiritual integrity of the church, but a process of correction running afoul. An individual member of the church done harm by another is told to deal with the problem personally, by confronting the offender (18:15). But what if this does not work? "If he refuses to listen," then the church's decision is required (18:17). We see how the community is called upon to decide when the personal process fails. The church does not decide all cases, but the cases which affect all.

An intermediate step is found in the two or three witnesses who accompany the offended party and try to resolve the matter with the offender (18:16). These represent the larger community. At least implicit reference is made to the Scripture as warrant for the church's practice, for the use of two or three witnesses recalls Deut. 19:15 (as it did in 1 Tim. 5:19). The process moves in stages from the individual to the communal.

Only if the offender does not heed these witnesses is the story told to the assembly as a whole. For the first time in these fragmentary texts, we see the function of *narrative* in the decision-making process. The narration (by the offended person? by the witnesses?) forms the basis for the community discernment and decision (Matt. 18:17). If the offender listens, the health of the church's processes is affirmed. But what if the man does not listen to the voice even of the church as a whole? Then he poses a direct threat to the community's right to reach decision. Such a frontal attack on the church's authority to decide its future and discipline its members can only be met by excommunication, for the survival of the group is at stake. Failed discipline leads logically to exclusion: "Let him be to you as a Gentile and tax collector" (18:17). As in the case of the Corinthian excommunication, the assembly is gathered in the name of Jesus and has the power of Jesus present to it (18:20). For this reason, when the community reaches "agreement" (18:19), its decisions are "binding" with God (18:18).

Neither the Pauline nor Matthean passage directly addresses the question, "How should the church go about making decision?" But from the specific cases of deviance and defiance leading to excommunication, we can deduce some of the implied norms of these communities which are made explicit by the decision-making process. The assembly is clearly more than a collection of like-minded folk. When it is gathered in Jesus's name, the assembly is visited by the power of the Lord—the Holy Spirit.

The church does not meet to replace individual discernment—the responsibility of each member—but to address challenges posed to the group's life as a whole—challenges only the group can meet. The reaching of decision requires the assertion of the community's identity. It may call for the invocation, and therefore rereading, of Scripture.

1 Corinthians 12-14

At this point, we should look at another passage in 1 Corinthians, where similar dynamics are found. Paul does not deal with the process of decision making at all in 1 Corinthians 12-14, but with another way the church articulates its life. The setting is worship, and the problem is the proper use of spiritual gifts in the assembly. This is a church richly gifted by the Spirit in knowledge and speech (1 Cor. 1:5), able not only to proclaim by the Spirit "Jesus is Lord" (12:3), but to express that confession in diverse ministries of speech (12:4-11), especially tongues and prophecy. For our purposes, we need only note some aspects of Paul's elaborate argument.

First, we see that all ministries make explicit what is implied in the life of the community as a whole. Thus, Paul emphasizes that the Spirit of unity is the giver of diverse gifts (12:11), and that no ministry makes sense apart from the body of which it is a part and serves (12:14-31). Second, we learn that Paul prefers the gift of prophecy to that of tongues—though he acknowledges that gift (14:5) and even uses it (14:18)—for definite reasons. Prophecy uses the mind in a way tongues do not (14:13-19). As a result, prophecy builds up the *community* in faith, whereas tongues edify only the one praying (14:4, 12, 17-19, 26). "Edification" is a strong term for Paul, fundamental to his understanding of the church as a "temple of God" (3:16). Building the church is an apostolic activity directed by God (3:10-15), and prophecy advances it. For this reason, prophecy ranks next to apostleship in Paul's lists of spiritual gifts (1 Cor. 12:28; Eph. 2:20; cf. Rom. 12:6). Paul also wants tongues to be interpreted, so that they too can build up the church's faith (1 Cor. 14:5). If there is no interpretation available, tongue-speakers should be silent (14:28). Speech within the assembly, we see, is to be an articulation of faith. Prophecy reveals to the community the implications of its response to God, the demands of the gospel here and now. This is the point of Paul's lengthy illustration in 1 Cor. 14:20-25. When the gospel's demands are clearly enunciated by prophecy within the assembly, even unbelievers who enter are convinced and convicted, and moved to the confession that God is present in the community (14:25). Ecstatic utterance alone, however, can be understood as just another form of religious ranting, with none of the gospel to it (14:23).

The third thing to notice about this passage is Paul's concern for order and peace in the assembly. It is contrary to the nature of God's Spirit that there should be competitive jostling for the chance to speak (14:33). Those with spiritual gifts should take turns to speak (14:27-29). Even in the most "charismatic" group there is need for order, and being led by the spirit does not exclude the necessity for human choice. We see that Paul insists on this: "The spirits of prophets are subject to prophets" (14:32). This cryptic statement can mean two things. Paul clearly understands that the norms for prophecy are not external and legal, but internal and spiritual. He also means that the prophets are capable of rationally directing their utterance, able to observe the proper order in the assembly.

The most fascinating feature of this passage for our discussion is Paul's insistence that everyone in the assembly has the responsibility of *discerning* the utterances of those who speak publicly. In 1 Cor. 14:29, he says, "Let two or three prophets speak, and let the others weigh what is said." Two possible misunderstandings of the English should be clarified by reference to the Greek text. Although Paul's usage is not consistent enough to make it absolutely certain, the weight of evidence, and particularly his statement in 1 Cor. 14:37, indicates that by "others" Paul does not simply mean "other prophets," but everyone in the assembly. The translation "let them weigh," furthermore, is somewhat weak. Paul uses this word (*diakrinō*) elsewhere to mean a kind of "judgment" which can best be translated as "discernment" (cf. Rom. 14:23; 1 Cor. 6:5; 11:29). The whole community, therefore, should discern prophetic utterance and the interpretation of tongues. Indeed, in 1 Cor. 12:10, after the gift of prophecy Paul lists the gift to "distinguish between [i.e., discern] spirits." This is no more an exclusive gift than that of faith (cf. 12:9). As with all spiritual ministries, Paul regards those specially gifted as articulating implicit aspects of the church's life. As with prophecy, so with discernment.

It is by such discernment that the church can "test the spirits"(1 John 4:1). Only because all have the Spirit of God and have been gifted with the "mind of Christ" (1 Cor. 2:16) can each decide on the adequacy or appropriateness of prophetic speech within the assembly. That this is indeed a demand made on all is shown by 1 Cor. 14:37, where Paul says that anyone claiming to be a prophet or spiritual person but not recognizing the authority of Paul's instructions—that they are "from the Lord"—is not acknowledged by the community. The spiritual gift of discernment is the necessary companion of public speech within the church, both in worship and in the reaching of decisions.

Galatians 2:1-10

A final passage from Paul demands our attention, and provides a transition to those fuller narrative passages whose peculiar problems we must next face. This passage is also a narrative, albeit a highly charged one. In Gal. 2:1-10, Paul reports a decision reached by him and the leaders of the Jerusalem Church—James, Cephas, John. The agreement was sealed by "the right hand of fellowship" between Paul and Barnabas on one side, and the Jerusalem leaders on the other (Gal. 2:9). The Jerusalem leaders agreed on the legitimacy of Paul's preaching to Gentiles, and on the inclusion of Gentiles in the church. They recognized that in both Peter's ministry to the circumcised and Paul's to the uncircumcised, *God* had been at work (2:8). In deciding for the inclusion of the Gentiles, therefore, they decided for God. The Jewish Christian leaders recognized that the mission of Paul and Barnabas resulted from a grace given by God (2:9).

Most remarkable in this short report is the basis for the decision. Paul says he went up because of a vision, and "I laid before them (but privately before those who were of repute) the gospel which I preach among the Gentiles" (2:2). The Greek verb "lay before" has the sense of "submit," but also (as in Acts 25:14), the sense of "relate, communicate." It is precisely Paul's narration, his telling of what he did and taught among the Gentiles, which allowed the other leaders to discern that this was God's work.

The human elements of the story are all too evident. The polemic, however, cannot hide a process of decision making in the church of the first generation which made conscious acknowledgment of the transcendent context for its life (Gal. 2:2, 6, 8, 9), which allowed for a challenge potentially threatening to the group to be expressed in a narrative of faith (2:2), and which led to decision on the basis of discerning God's work active in the lives of others. This account by Paul brings us to the most ex-

tended passage dealing with decision making in the primitive Church, Acts
15:1–35.

A Narrative Text: Acts 15:1–35

This passage takes up virtually an entire chapter in the Acts of the
Apostles, the second volume of the work often referred to as Luke-Acts.
It narrates that critical event of the early church, sometimes called the
Apostolic Council. This account, as we shall see later, is itself the climax
to a series of other passages pertinent to our discussion. Even taken alone,
it is unique in the New Testament for the fullness of the attention it gives
to the decision-making process. The problems it presents for theological
appropriation have to do with its being a narrative.

¹But some men came down from Judea and were teaching the brethren,
"Unless you are circumcised according to the custom of Moses, you cannot
be saved." ²And when Paul and Barnabas had no small dissension and debate
with them, Paul and Barnabas and some of the others were appointed to go
up to Jerusalem to the apostles and the elders about this question. ³So, being
sent on their way by the church, they passed through both Phoenicia and
Samaria, reporting the conversion of the Gentiles, and they gave great joy
to all the brethren. ⁴When they came to Jerusalem, they were welcomed by
the church and the apostles and the elders, and they declared all that God had
done with them. ⁵But some of the believers who belonged to the party of the
Pharisees rose up, and said, "It is necessary to circumcise them, and to charge
them to keep the law of Moses."

⁶The apostles and the elders were gathered together to consider this matter. ⁷And after there had been much debate, Peter rose and said to them,
"Brethren, you know that in the early days God made choice among you,
that by my mouth the Gentiles should hear the word of the gospel and believe.
⁸And God who knows the heart bore witness to them, giving them the Holy
Spirit just as he did to us; ⁹and he made no distinction between us and them,
but cleansed their hearts by faith. ¹⁰Now therefore why do you make trial of
God by putting a yoke upon the neck of the disciples which neither our fathers
nor we have been able to bear? ¹¹But we believe that we shall be saved through
the grace of the Lord Jesus, just as they will."

¹²And all the assembly kept silence; and they listened to Barnabas and Paul
as they related what signs and wonders God had done through them among
the Gentiles. ¹³After they finished speaking, James replied, "Brethren, listen
to me. ¹⁴Simeon has related how God first visited the Gentiles, to take out
of them a people for his name. ¹⁵And with this the words of the prophets agree,
as it is written,

[16]'After this I will return,
  and I will rebuild the dwelling of
    David, which has fallen;
  I will rebuild its ruins,
  and I will set it up,
[17]that the rest of men may seek the
    Lord,
  and all the Gentiles who are called
    by my name,
[18]says the Lord, who has made these
    things known from of old.'
[19]Therefore my judgment is that we should not trouble those of the Gentiles who turn to God, [20]but should write to them to abstain from the pollutions of idols and from unchastity and from what is strangled and from blood. [21]For from early generations Moses has had in every city those who preach him, for he is read every sabbath in the synagogues.''

[22]Then it seemed good to the apostles and elders, with the whole church, to choose men from among them and send them to Antioch with Paul and Barnabas. They sent Judas called Barsabbas, and Silas, leading men among the brethren, [23]with the following letter: ''The brethren, both the apostles and the elders, to the brethren who are of the Gentiles in Antioch and Syria and Cilicia, greeting. [24]Since we have heard that some persons from us have troubled you with words, unsettling your minds, although we gave them no instructions, [25]it has seemed good to us, having come to one accord, to choose men and send them to you with our beloved Barnabas and Paul, [26] men who have risked their lives for the sake of our Lord Jesus Christ. [27]We have therefore sent Judas and Silas, who themselves will tell you the same things by word of mouth. [28]For it has seemed good to the Holy Spirit and to us to lay upon you no greater burden than these necessary things: [29]that you abstain from what has been sacrificed to idols and from blood and from what is strangled and from unchastity. If you keep yourselves from these, you will do well. Farewell.''

[30]So when they were sent off, they went down to Antioch; and having gathered the congregation together, they delivered the letter. [31]And when they read it, they rejoiced at the exhortation. [32]And Judas and Silas, who were themselves prophets, exhorted the brethren with many words and strengthened them. [33]And after they had spent some time, they were sent off in peace by the brethren to those who had sent them. [35]But Paul and Barnabas remained in Antioch, teaching and preaching the word of the Lord, with many others also.

Given the generally overgrown state of New Testament scholarship, one might suppose that the possible pertinence of Acts 15 to anything would have been noticed by now, and certainly its relevance to the process by which the church reaches its decisions. But a survey of what has been written on the passage over the past several decades shows a remarkably narrow range of interest in it.

The Use of Acts 15

Among those working within the guild of New Testament scholarship, the passage has been studied from the point of view of several "criticisms." The text-critical question has stirred some interest, because of the characteristic and extensive variants (Codex D at 15:20 and 15:29 inserts the "Golden Rule" among the other parts of the decree). Others have asked the source-critical question: what if anything in this passage goes back to previous sources, and how has the final editor reworked them? The greatest amount of attention has been given to the historical-critical question, namely the relation between this passage and Galatians 2 which, as we have seen, also reports a meeting between Paul and the Jerusalem leaders, but in quite a different manner. The historical issues of chronology, accuracy, and bias are raised by the apparent conflict, if not contradiction, between the two reports.

In particular, the reality or fate of the so-called apostolic decree (Acts 15:23–29) has proven a knotty problem. If there really was such a decree, why didn't Paul, in his discussion of meats offered to idols in 1 Cor. 8–10, refer to it? Was he actually in disagreement with it? Was there a decree at all, or did Luke make it up? Or did the decree have only a regional application (in Antioch, Syria, Cilicia according to Acts 15:23) and not necessarily apply in Corinth? Some attention has also been given to the thematic role played by James's discourse in 15:14–21, as well as to the influence this narrative had in the formation of the "conciliar idea" in early Christianity. That these historical questions have preoccupied New Testament scholars is neither particularly surprising nor reprehensible. Until very recently, New Testament scholarship often thought of itself as basically a historical enterprise.

It is a bit more surprising to discover the neglect of Acts 15 in theological works devoted expressly to the church. Especially in an era when "world" and "ecumenical" councils have generated so much theological reflection, Acts 15 would seem the perfect text to exploit as a paradigm. There is no end to what is written, of course, and I may have missed even significant contributions, but my own reading in the area has not yielded any serious appropriation of Acts 15 by theological discussion. The references I have found tend to be casual and somewhat *pro forma*, even in writings specifically dealing with the conciliar ideal. Why haven't theologians used this passage?

Doctrinal theologians try to work with biblical material as mediated to them by biblical scholars. The constantly changing face of biblical *scholarship* has created the impression, even among theologians, that only those professionally trained in that field can possibly excavate the texts of the Bible. New Testament scholars, in turn, have been using the historical-critical method in their investigations. Historical methods can ask only historical questions, which can receive only historical answers. Consequently, the data supplied theologians by biblical scholars has tended to take the form of historical information. In theological works on the church, for example, we find that Acts is used as a source of information about the forms of ministry in the early church, but it appears to offer little else for theological reflection.

The dominance of the historical method has had a powerful effect on the theological appropriation of biblical texts. Some unspoken assumptions exercise considerable influence. One of these is that "history" is itself the vehicle of theology, so that the "historical" form of the early church has critical theological relevance for the contemporary church—if we can but reconstruct it. Another assumption is that the methods of historical inquiry can function as theological criteria. We can see this assumption at work when theologians use the conclusions of historians on the dating, authorship, and authenticity of New Testament writings as norms for their *theological* worth. Luke-Acts, for example, is conventionally regarded as a writing coming from the second Christian generation. Since that generation is seen as one in which the earliest "charismatic" structure of the church had become routinized and institutionalized, Luke-Acts must be reading back into its account of the first generation these outlooks of the second. This portrait of the church, therefore, "must" be one in which the Spirit is demoted and tradition has replaced enthusiasm. The picture of the church in Luke-Acts betrays the picture of the church in Paul. There is little either in Paul's letters or Luke-Acts to support these opinions, however widely they are held. What is remarkable, however, is that they are not only held by scholars doing history, but by those doing theology as well.

Acts 15 also has been studied from the viewpoint of biblical theology, especially as found in works on "the church in the New Testament." The intention to do theology in biblical terms is laudable, but in practice, biblical theology has often been little more than an archeological dig. The result has been that the biblical witness remains firmly in the past, even further removed from contemporary theological appropriation. Insofar as "New Testament theology," for example, has attempted to establish some unity among the obviously diverse New Testament writings, it has done so at the cost either of *harmonizing* them, or *selecting* some as more normative than others. Both moves betray the canonical principle, which asserts the normative importance of all the witnesses precisely in their diversity. Furthermore, the attempts to describe a "biblical world view" in general or on particular topics has only accentuated the distance between that world and ours, for it has led to the impression that each is a fixed "thing." Finally, much of what is done from this perspective amounts to a series of "theologies of": the "theology of Paul" or the "theology of Luke." This sort of descriptive appreciation is not yet theology. The chapter given to Luke-Acts in New Testament studies of the church (ecclesiologies) concentrates on the Lukan notions of ministry. These notions are accounted for by the supposed historical situation and, therefore, the Lukan theological perceptions. In short, whether in technical New Testament scholarship, or in doctrinal or biblical theology, Acts 15 has been appropriated through the categories of history: the history of the text— with Luke as source; the history of ideas—with Luke the thinker studied.

The Historical Difficulty

Another aspect of this historical fixation is a preoccupation with *what* Luke says to the neglect of *how* he says it. Information yielded by the narrative is considered important; the shape of the narrative is not. The failure to read Acts 15 as a narrative with theological implications does not result from discrimination against this passage alone. It comes from a long-standing and pervasive neglect of biblical narratives both in Scripture studies and in theology. Recently, "literary" approaches to the New Testament appear to be reversing the trend. Such studies, however, have devoted far more attention to shorter narratives than to longer ones, and have concentrated more on aesthetic than on theological dimensions of the text. Few bridges have been thrown across the gap separating the realm of narrative from the realm of theological reflection, and none in the case of Acts 15.

But let us suppose a theologian wants to use the narrative of Acts 15 as a source for theological reflection on the church. Isn't the attempt futile, given the doubtful historicity of the story, and its apparent tendentiousness? If the story is not historically accurate, in other words, does it have any value for the church—as a historical community—in its process of seeking to understand itself and the one who calls it? We find ourselves at a critical juncture. If the theological use of a narrative text depends on its historical accuracy, we limit the narrative's range of meaning to the referential. It is the action of the past we consider meaningful; the narrative has worth only insofar as it accurately reports that event. Or perhaps it has some derivative interest as witness to the author's perception of the event. In either case, historicity becomes the touchstone of narrative worth.

The question of historicity is something of a false issue in the case of the Apostolic Council, anyway. Only the most acute case of historicism would lead someone to deny that behind the different and sometimes conflicting reports of Luke (Acts 15) and Paul (Galations 2) there was a real and significant series of events. The discrepancies in the two sources are of interest, after all, only because of their general agreement. Something happened. Very early on in the life of the church there was a crisis stimulated by the conversion of non-Jews to belief in Jesus as Messiah and Lord. Gentiles, entering a community which till then had seen itself as the faithful remnant of God's people Israel, posed a challenge to the church's self-understanding. The church had to decide on the legitimacy of this Gentile mission. If that be granted, it had to decide what conditions would be required of them to be considered part of the people. The question came down to whether there would be one or two churches. To settle the matter, at least one meeting was held in Jerusalem—acknowledged by all participants as the mother church—where these issues were raised and discussed. Peter, Paul, James, and Barnabas all certainly took an active and important part. They reached a decision in amicable fashion. They remained in fellowship. Both sources regard the decision as having the most fundamental and far-reaching consequences.

Questions, of course, remain. Was there only one meeting, or more than one? Do the sources refer to the same or different meetings? Did Paul go to Jerusalem as part of an Antiochean delegation (Acts), or in response to personal revelation (Galatians)? Did Titus accompany Paul (Galatians), or not? Did this meeting precede or follow the stormy encounter between Paul and Cephas at Antioch where table-fellowship was also the issue? Acts makes a conflict at Antioch the cause of the Council. But Paul locates the conflict with ''certain men from James'' and Cephas after the Jerusalem meeting. Was the decision of the leaders formulated in a ''decree'' (Acts)? Was part of the agreement that Paul and Barnabas should take up a collection (Galatians)? These are legitimate issues and remain grounds for further investigation. But by the standards of sane historiography, there is much more certain here than uncertain.

Then, what about Luke's narrative? There are two main options. The first is that things happened the way he says they did, and he accurately records them. A corollary of this is that Paul is either talking about another meeting, or, deliberately or not, gives a mistaken account. High regard for Paul should not automatically rule out the possibility of his being slightly tendentious, as well. In this first option, Luke's account and history would coincide. The second option is that things happened in quite a different fashion than the way Luke describes them, that is, either as Paul has it, or in a manner altogether different from both sources. Luke, however, reports them the way he does for one of three reasons: a) his sources are deficient or wrong; b) he wishes to correct another version he regards as erroneous or one-sided; c) consciously or not, he wishes to idealize the event, in order to teach the church. In this option, Luke writes with less concern for ''what actually happened'' than for ''what should have happened.''

For the sake of argument, let us take the second option as the most likely: deliberately or not, Luke idealized the event. We are, in other words, at the furthest remove from what is usually regarded as accurate historical reporting. If our theological reflection depends on the absolute historical accuracy of the narrative, we can go no further. Although Luke reports ''something'' that happened, the way he tells it distorts the event, and his narrative in its details, therefore, is useless. But another attitude towards Luke's narrative is possible. We can regard Luke as a divinely inspired teacher of the church, through whose narrative both the community of his day and the church of our day are authoritatively addressed by God.

Now we are free to ask not *whether*, but in what *way* Luke's narrative might be normative for us in our reflection on the life of the church. We can allow his narrative to become for us, as it was for him, the vehicle of theology.

The Literary Difficulty

The shift comes in hearing Luke not first of all as a poor historian or even creative theologian whose perceptions may or may not be accurate, but as a prophetic witness, through whose words God's Word can be heard by believers. By being included in the canon, Luke's writing as *writing* has been certified by the community as a witness which speaks not only to its own time but to every time of the church, not only in its human voice, but in God's voice as well. I stress that it is not *history* which has been canonized and is therefore normative. *Texts* are canonized and therefore stand as normative. It is not the reconstructed course of development in the early church which speaks to us, a reconstruction dependent on texts, but the writings given birth by the development which still speak today. Reading Luke-Acts in this way does not derive from the decisions of scholarship, but the decisions of faith within the church. When we allow the narrative itself to question us and our understanding, we listen to the voice of the prophet.

The shift, however, demands that we face another question. Is it genuinely the prophet's voice to which we attend, or only ours, projected unto the text? Even if we are not "doing history," isn't the "historical meaning" of the text necessary to maintain, if we are not to fly off into fancifulness? Yes, it is, but properly understood. The "historical meaning" of the text does not refer to the historical situation it addressed, but to the historical conditioning of the language of the text. Especially when these writings are read by a historical community which looks to them for its self-understanding, it is important that this literal, or historical, meaning of the text be the framework for the search. This conviction has long been held by Protestants, and was given magisterial expression for the Catholic Church in the Second Vatican Council's *Decree on Divine Revelation* III, 12:

> However, since God speaks in sacred Scripture through men in human fashion, the interpreter of sacred Scripture, in order to see clearly what God wanted to communicate to us, should carefully investigate what meaning the sacred writers really intended and what God wanted to manifest by their words.

Some contemporary literary critics are uncomfortable with the notion of "author's intention," thinking that it raises the impossible task of finding out what was in the author's head when he wrote and limits the meaning of a text which, once released from the pen, begins a life of its own apart from the will of the writer. But so long as we do not confuse the philosophical notion of "intention" with psychological factors like "motivation" and "purpose," the concept of the author's intention is both necessary and helpful. After all, until a text *does* leave a writer's hand it is in an organic and causal relationship with the writer in a way it is not to any reader. The text bears the marks of an author in a way different from the creative tracings of readers.

At any rate, the point of "intention" is not what was in the author's head, but what the author put on paper. If a text does not bear the impress of the author's thought and imagination, then it is not properly a "writing" at all. In poetry, worry about intentional fallacies may be in order. But it is overly fastidious in narratives which at least purport to give accounts of real events. Finally, the point of respecting the author's intention, insofar as it is discernable in the text, is not to prohibit further meanings which new readers might discover, but to limit them to those which are consonant with the nature of the text. To ignore the historical linguistic conditioning of a text, therefore, is to subvert the text's ability to mediate a historical community's tradition.

If we are to discover Luke's intention, it can only be through the text itself. If we had some independent testimony from him as to what he wanted to say, it would not matter, unless he *did* in fact say it. Even then, it would be only another reader's opinion. To speak of the author's intention is in effect to look for the structure of the writing, its way of saying what it says. The meaning of a narrative, moreover, cannot be extracted from the text itself as a sort of residue. It inheres in the text as text. This means that not a summation or proposition, but the text itself must continue to be read. The text shows its meaning fully as much in its "form" as in its "content." Indeed, the categories are hard to distinguish. This is true for all narratives, and is definitely the case in Luke-Acts, where the question about the author's intention must be answered in terms of the shape of the story.

The more the method of Luke is uncovered by careful readers of his writing, the more convincing becomes the case that Luke intended his story as a whole to be the vehicle for his witness to the church. Study of the so-called "summaries" in Acts (e.g. 2:41–47; 4:32–37; 5:12–16) has shown that Luke tends to idealize, with an eye toward edification, situations historically more complex than his narrative would suggest. Analysis of the speeches in Acts (e.g. 2:14–36; 7:2–53; 13:16–41; 17:22–31) has led to a similar conclusion. Whatever traditional elements he uses in them, the perspective and placement of these speeches admirably serve Luke's narrative goals. The summaries and speeches serve a paradigmatic purpose. What is true of these smaller units is also true for his story as a whole. The overall structure of Luke's story is critical to his purpose. Scholars have observed that Luke's careful formulation of the prologue to the Gospel expresses succinctly what he has actually accomplished in the writing. He tells his reader Theophilus that he wants to provide him with security or assurance concerning the things in which he had already been instructed (Luke 1:4). How will he accomplish this? By telling the story of how God has fulfilled his promises "in order" (*kathexēs*; RSV "orderly account," Luke 1:3). "In order" is an especially revealing term. The sequence of the story is significant in Luke-Acts to a remarkable degree. How one thing follows after another seems almost as important as the things themselves. This is because the ordered form of memory itself has a convincing quality. If, therefore, the story of Luke-Acts is the means by which his literary and theological goals are met, then the story line is equally important for the appropriation of Luke-Acts by theological reflection. The story is the voice of this witness. The story the author tells is itself, as story, a *datum* of theology.

The Theological Difficulty

The force of this proposition may become clearer when we seriously ask theological questions about the Apostolic Council as it is described in Acts 15. Wherein does it have significance for the church today, if it has any? Does it consist in the information it gives about church order (apostles and elders) in the early Christian community—if Luke is accurately reporting and not reading them back from his own time? Perhaps a theologian could use this relatively less complex system as a reproach to a rigid hierarchical structure. That would be a helpful critical use. But the narrative is thereby reduced to supplying information, and information clearly of only secondary interest to the author himself. In this case, there would be no connection between theological appropriation and the literary shape of the text.

Is it, then, the actual decision of the Council which retains normative force for the church today? If we take the wording of the decree literally, "that you abstain from what has been sacrificed to idols and from blood and from what is strangled and from unchastity" (Acts 15:29), it seems unlikely. The chastity part we might agree with, but few would argue that Christians should return to eating meat slaughtered only under kosher regulations. In fact, the textual variants of the decree testify to the checkered career it had in churches where Acts 15 was read. No, the content of the decree appears to stay fixed in the past, representing an important step in the development of the church, but no longer of critical relevance.

Perhaps the theological significance of the Council rests on the principles enunciated by some of its participants, such as that spoken by Peter in 15:11: "We shall be saved through the grace of the Lord Jesus, just as they will." This is a statement of great importance. Taken with the still sharper sayings of Paul on the radical breakdown of human distinctions in Christ (e.g. 1 Cor. 7:17–24; 12:13; Gal. 3:27–29; Eph. 2:11–22; Col. 3:11), it stands as an enduring norm against which the church can measure itself. The principle, however, is found elsewhere, and, abstracted from the narrative, represents only a fraction of the passage's meaning.

What, then? I suggest that the prophetic witness of the Acts 15 narrative is critical to the theological reflection of the church because it gives the fullest picture in the New Testament of the process by which the church reaches decision. Only in Acts do we find a sustained treatment of the *process* by which the primitive church did or should have decided its future as God's people. Only here do we have so explicit a picture of the church as *church* articulating its faith in response to new and threatening circumstances. Furthermore, it is only in the narrative as *narrative* that this process is to be found. Acts 15 witnesses to the church concerning the way it reaches decisions, not by prescription, but by way of a paradigmatic story.

The church is not called on by its hearing of this witness to imitate mechanically the steps taken by the characters in the story. The narrative, rather, invites us to consider the dynamics of decision making themselves, and to use this consideration when reflecting on the contemporary practice of the church wherever it exists. This narrative provides the theologian within the church with another and authoritative witness to the essential qualities necessary for the church to remain church as it decides hard questions.

A theological reading of Acts 15 would allow the biblical narrative to speak to the narratives of our own experience and self–understanding, that is, to pose the critical and interpretative questions to our own practices and presuppositions. The dynamics of the biblical story are to inform and, possibly, reform our own. The hearing of the biblical story, in short, should help us more keenly hear our own; the telling of the biblical story should give us the capacity to tell our own. We now turn to the hearing part of the task.

Bibliographical Note

For the sort of work done by New Testament scholars asking technical questions, one can begin with the commentary and helpful bibliography in Ernst Haenchen, *The Acts of the Apostles: A Commentary*, Eng. trans. B. Noble (Philadelphia: Westminster Press, 1971). The neglect of Acts 15 in the theology of the church can be seen, by way of example, in Hans Küng, *The Church* (New York: Doubleday & Co., 1976), and Jürgen Moltmann, *The Church in the Power of the Spirit* (New York: Harper & Row, 1978). Both writers also demonstrate the use of historical data to make theological judgments on Luke-Acts; so Küng, p. 238, and Moltmann, p. 298. Representative of scholarship on "the church in the New Testament" are the monographs of Eduard Schweizer, *Church Order in the New Testament*, Studies in Biblical Theology 32 (London: SCM Press, 1961) and Rudolf Schnackenburg, *The Church in the New Testament*, Eng. trans. W. J. O'Hara (New York: Herder & Herder, 1965). The hopes and disappointments of "biblical theology" are well chronicled by Brevard Childs, *Biblical Theology in Crisis* (Philadelphia: Westminster Press, 1970). An instructive study of the neglect of narrative in the guild of biblical scholarship is Hans Frei's *The Eclipse of Biblical Narrative: A Study in Eighteenth and Nineteenth Century Hermeneutics* (New Haven, Conn.: Yale University Press, 1974). For a stimulating discussion of the choices certain theologians have made regarding the authoritative use of Scripture, See David Kelsey, *The Uses of Scripture in Recent Theology* (Philadelphia: Fortress Press, 1975), and his more constructive theological proposal, "The Bible and Christian Theology," *The Journal of the American Academy of Religion* 48 (1980): 385–402. On the literary methods of Luke, cf. Luke T. Johnson, *The Literary Function of Possessions in Luke-Acts* (Missoula, Mont.: Scholars Press, 1977). A fuller bibliographical support for this chapter can be found in my unpublished paper submitted to the Luke-Acts Task Force of the Catholic Biblical Association in 1978, "The Use of Acts 15 in the Theology of the Church: A Scouting Report."

3

DECISIONS

I have dealt only with the problems facing a theological interpretation of Acts 15. The same sort of considerations apply to the other narratives in Acts showing the church reaching decision (Acts 1:15-26; 4:23-31; 6:1-6; 9:26-30), which are less full and have received even less attention. In this chapter, I will first look at these shorter passages, since they precede Acts 15 and anticipate some of its important elements. When I return to Acts 15, I will consider it as part of a longer story, extending from the conversion of Cornelius to the end of the Apostolic Council (10:1-15:35). The cross-references in 15:7 and 15:24 to earlier events makes this procedure necessary. Acts 15 is the climax to a complex plot. Before looking at any of these narrative passages, however, it is helpful to place them within the outlook of Luke-Acts on decisions generally, for their very presence in a work so dominated by divine direction is somewhat startling.

Divine Guidance and Human Decisions in Acts

Of all the characters who crowd the pages of Luke-Acts, God is the most active and dominant, directing the actions of the human figures. The prominence of God's guidance is not surprising, since Luke was trying to show how God fulfilled the promises through the things which had happened. The place for human freedom sometimes seems small. Many of the stages of the gospel's progress to Rome, for example, take place under God's direct impulse. Thus, the angel of God releases Peter and John from prison to preach (5:19-21), and Peter from imprisonment a second time (12:6-17). The angel of the Lord and the Spirit guide Philip (8:26, 29, 39). The Holy Spirit selects Paul and Barnabas for mission in Antioch (13:1-3), forbids Paul's preaching in Asia (16:6-7), and drives Paul to his fateful journey to Jerusalem (20:22). Peter and John state the force of the divine direction succinctly when they declare that they cannot but proclaim (4:20) and must obey God rather than men (5:29).

Other stages of the mission seem generated by circumstances arranged by God. Those scattered by persecution from Jerusalem preach in Samaria (8:4) and to the Hellenists in Antioch (11:19–21). In response, the Jerusalem leaders send Peter and John to confirm the Samaritan mission (8:14) and Barnabas the mission in Antioch (11:22). When Paul's preaching of Jesus as Messiah is rejected by Jews, he simply turns to the Gentiles, seeing in this the fulfillment of the Scripture (cf. 13:46–47; 18:6; 28:25–28).

The narrative sometimes shows some interplay between human decision–or indecisiveness–and divine direction. Paul decided to go to Damascus to persecute "the Way," but is overturned and transformed (9:3ff). Ananias's hesitancy to receive Paul is countered by a reassuring revelation (9:10–16). The decision of Paul to go to Macedonia is triggered by a vision (16:9–10). On the other side, Paul is told by the Spirit not to go to Jerusalem (21:4) and warned by prophecy what would face him there (21:11), but he still goes. Paul and Barnabas decide to part company on purely personal grounds, disagreeing over John-Mark (15:37–40). Finally, there is the short account of the disciples in Antioch collecting money for Jerusalem in response to prophecy (11:27–30).

With the partial exception of the last, these passages do not show us the church as *church* reaching decision. If we had only these texts, we could learn that God intervenes in special ways to effect his will, and that negative circumstances can turn out to be stages in the working out of God's plan. But we would learn nothing of how the human church might go about making decisions God had not already made for it.

Four Cases of the Church Making Decision

In contrast, four passages in Acts show us the assembly acting as a group, and reaching decision as a group. In each case the narrative discloses some aspects of the decision-making process.

The Election of Matthias (Acts 1:15–26)

[15]In those days Peter stood up among the brethren (the company of persons was in all about a hundred and twenty), and said, [16]"Brethren, the scripture had to be fulfilled, which the Holy Spirit spoke beforehand by the mouth

of David, concerning Judas who was guide to those who arrested Jesus. [17]For he was numbered among us, and was allotted his share in this ministry. [18](Now this man bought a field with the reward of his wickedness; and falling headlong he burst open in the middle and all his bowels gushed out. [19]And it became known to all the inhabitants of Jerusalem, so that the field was called in their language Akeldama, that is, Field of Blood.) [20]For it is written in the book of Psalms,

'Let his habitation become desolate,
and let there be no one to live in it';
and
'His office let another take.'

[21]So one of the men who have accompanied us during all the time that the Lord Jesus went in and out among us, [22]beginning from the baptism of John until the day when he was taken up from us—one of these men must become with us a witness to his resurrection.'' [23]And they put forward two, Joseph called Barsabbas, who was surnamed Justus, and Matthias. [24]And they prayed and said, ''Lord, who knowest the hearts of all men, show which one of these two thou hast chosen [25]to take the place in this ministry and apostleship from which Judas turned aside, to go to his own place.'' [26]And they cast lots for them, and the lot fell on Matthias, and he was enrolled with the eleven apostles.

Jesus has ascended (1:6–11), having promised that the Holy Spirit would come on his followers (Luke 24:49; Acts 1:5). Those who came up from Galilee with Jesus were gathered in the upper room (Acts 1:13), where they ''with one accord devoted themselves to prayer'' (1:14) and waited for the Spirit. Before it comes, though, Luke shows us the assembly deliberating. Two issues need settling. Should Judas be replaced, and if so, by whom? The placement of this passage before Pentecost (2:1ff) is important. By reaching this decision now, the community articulates its identity as *Israel*. The apostasy of Judas is significant because it broke the symbolic circle of the Twelve, who represent the restored Israel upon which the Spirit is to fall. That Judas's defection was seen as something more than a personal sin, indeed as a threat to the group, tells us something about the church's identity.

Peter's narrative dominates the passage. It is structured by the double ''must'' of 1:16 and 1:22. He first tells how the Scripture ''had to be fulfilled.'' How? By telling the story of Judas's defection. Then he proposes the selection of a replacement, one who ''must'' become a witness of the resurrection. It is Peter's narrative which forms the basis for the proposal and the decision. The narrative does not baldly recite facts, but interprets the very psalm verses it invokes for authority. Peter cites verses of two psalms (Ps. 69:25, 109:8) which are found together only here in the New Testament. We see narrative and scriptural interpretation interpenetrate. Judas's apostasy is bracketed by "had to be fulfilled" and the citations themselves. The words of David are "concerning Judas." Peter's rereading reveals implications of the text never anticipated by its author. The decision to replace Judas is based on a theological interpretation of the event of his betrayal.

The prayer of the community contains another small, interpretative narrative (1:24–25). The strangest aspect of this passage occurs in the reference to the casting of lots: it makes clear that although the community nominates, it is God who discerns the hearts of all who calls one to apostleship. The assembly has been active throughout: it has listened to Peter's narrative and proposal; it has nominated two men (both steps involving discernment); it has prayed, cast lots, and enrolled Matthias among the other apostles, thus affirming as a community the decision revealed by God. As leader, Peter has narrated, interpreted the Scripture, and proposed action.

The Decision to Continue Preaching (Acts 4:23–31)

[23]When they were released they went to their friends and reported what the chief priests and the elders had said to them. [24]And when they heard it, they lifted their voices together to God and said, "Sovereign Lord, who didst make the heaven and the earth and the sea and everything in them, [25]who by the mouth of our father David, thy servant, didst say by the Holy Spirit,
'Why did the Gentiles rage,
and the peoples imagine vain things?
[26]The kings of the earth set themselves
   in array,
and the rulers were gathered
   together,
against the Lord and against his
   Anointed'—
[27]for truly in this city there were gathered together against thy holy servant Jesus, whom thou didst anoint, both Herod and Pontius Pilate, with the Gentiles and the peoples of Israel, [28]to do whatever thy hand and thy plan had predestined to take place. [29]And now, Lord, look upon their threats, and grant to thy servants to speak thy word with all boldness, [30]while thou stretchest out thy hand to heal, and signs and wonders are performed through the name of thy holy servant Jesus. [31]And when they had prayed, the place in which

they were gathered together was shaken; and they were all filled with the Holy Spirit and spoke the word of God with boldness.

It may be questioned whether this narrative deals with the church reaching decision, on two counts. First, although the RSV translates the Greek in 4:23 as "their friends" (*pros tous idious*) this probably refers to the other apostles, rather than the whole assembly. Still, as we saw already in the Matthias story, the apostles represent the church as a whole in this part of Acts. The second difficulty is whether a decision is really made. It is at best implicit, though its consequences are clear.

The passage is a watershed in this part of Acts. Before it, Peter and John are arrested and told to preach no more in Jesus' name (4:17). After it, the apostles preach with even greater power, working signs and wonders among the people and within the assembly (4:32–5:16), so that the Sanhedrin, for fear of being stoned, dare not stop them (5:17–42). The challenge posed for the group is that of persecution: Should they go on preaching in Jesus' name? Peter and John already expressed their resolution (4:20), and now the group decides. It does so by the prayer for power in 4:24–30. The prayer is answered by an outpouring of the Spirit which enables them to proclaim with still greater force (4:33).

The community prays in response to the narrative. When they return to the group, Peter and John report on what had happened to them. In the prayer, narrative and scriptural interpretation once more intermingle. The community cites Ps. 2:1–2, which speaks of kings and rulers gathered against the Lord's anointed. The psalmist had obviously written about opponents of a Davidic king. In the prayer, however, the community applies it to the opposition shown Jesus, "whom thou didst anoint" (Acts 4:27). This application of the Old Testament to the sufferings of the Messiah is not exceptional in the New Testament. Far more striking, though, is the way *this* interpretation is then applied directly to the situation of the community. When *it* is persecuted, it remembers what Psalm 2 said about the sufferings of *Jesus*. This is not an automatic progression, but it is a remarkable one. The narrative of the community's experience extends the significance of the scriptural texts concerning the Messiah, so that they apply as well to the church of the Messiah. In the light of this, we are not surprised to find language otherwise applied to Jesus used in the prayer of the community for its own empowerment (4:29–30, cf. 2:22; 3:16). New experience leads to new understandings of texts, and therefore to a deeper self-understanding of the community itself. As in the election of Matthias, the community here listens to the narrative and prays. The leaders narrate and pray.

The Choosing of the Seven (Acts 6:1–6)

[1]Now in these days when the disciples were increasing in number, the Hellenists murmured against the Hebrews because their widows were neglected in the daily distribution. [2]And the twelve summoned the body of the disciples and said, ''It is not right that we should give up preaching the word of God to serve tables. [3]Therefore, brethren, pick out from among you seven men of good repute, full of the Spirit and of wisdom, whom we may appoint to this duty. [4]But we will devote ourselves to prayer and to the ministry of the word.'' [5]And what they said pleased the whole multitude, and they chose Stephen, a man full of faith and of the Holy Spirit, and Philip, and Prochorus, and Nicanor, and Timon, and Parmenas, and Nicolaus, a proselyte of Antioch. [6]These they set before the apostles, and they prayed and laid their hands upon them.

This decision comes after the second unsuccessful attempt by the Sanhedrin to stop the apostles' preaching, and the grudging recognition by one of its members, ''If it is of God, you will not be able to overthrow them'' (5:39). The very success of the movement, however, created new difficulties. Like all Jewish communities, early Christian communities exercised an organized form of assistance for the needy, especially orphans and widows. On a daily basis, there was something like a soup kitchen. The growth of the church among both Aramaic- and Greek-speaking synagogues within Jerusalem made this task complex and demanding. The ability of the apostles to continue overseeing the distribution of goods (cf. 4:35) was in doubt.

At an earlier stage, the distribution of possessions by the leaders served an important symbolic function for the community. It signified the reality and the style of apostolic authority (cf. 2:42–47, 4:32–37). The ministry of the word was closely joined, already by Jesus, to table-service (cf. Luke 9:10–17; 12:41–48; 22:24–30). The challenge facing the community, therefore, does not have to do simply with settling dissension. Nor does it concern the most efficient way to carry out a task, so that everyone's widows get fed. It involves a deeper identity issue, and concerns the nature of spiritual authority, its symbolization, and its transmission.

The multiplicity of factors at work in this passage makes it difficult to read at the level of historical inquiry. Ostensibly, the community decides who will care for widows among the Greek-speaking believers in Jerusalem. But in fact, the men appointed for the task never perform it; instead, just like the twelve, they go about preaching and performing wonders, only within a different constituency (cf. Acts 6:8, 8:5). The apparent inconsistency can best be accounted for by recognizing the symbolic nature of the decision. Appointing seven servants of the table for a different segment of the population symbolizes the transmission of spiritual authority to these men for another part of God's people, authority to preach and work wonders in the name of Jesus. In turn, the decision made by the church rendered more explicit its understanding of the apostolic office. It may have been symbolized by table-fellowship, but its essence was preaching (6:2), prayer, and the ministry of the word (6:4).

The process of reaching decision here bears some resemblance to the two previous passages: the assembly as a whole is gathered by the twelve (6:2), and there is a formal prayer by all before the laying on of hands (6:6). There is no narrative of experience here, only the simple statement of their proposal by the twelve. Nor is there any invocation of Scripture to interpret the situation. The role of the assembly is active. They discern the words of the twelve, and are "pleased" (6:5). The assembly chooses, literally "elects," those whom it recognizes as "full of the Spirit and of wisdom" (6:3) to be ministers, another act of discernment. These they place before the twelve. The Greek text does not make clear whether the whole assembly or only the twelve lay hands on the seven, and the evidence from elsewhere in Acts is too mixed for certainty either way (cf. 8:17–18; 9:17; 13:3; 19:6). At the least, the community listens, approves, chooses, and prays. The leaders state, propose, pray, and ordain.

The Acceptance of Paul as a Disciple (Acts 9:26–30)

[26]And when he had come to Jerusalem he attempted to join the disciples; and they were all afraid of him, for they did not believe that he was a disciple. [27]But Barnabas took him, and brought him to the apostles, and declared to them how on the road he had seen the Lord, who spoke to him, and how at Damascus he had preached boldly in the name of Jesus. [28]So he went in and out among them at Jerusalem, [29]preaching boldly in the name of the Lord. And he spoke and disputed against the Hellenists; but they were seeking to kill him. [30]And when the brethren knew it, they brought him down to Caesarea, and sent him off to Tarsus.

This brief account takes place after Paul's conversion (9:1–19) and after a short but stormy sojourn in Damascus (9:20–25). He returns to Jerusalem, not as a persecutor of "the Way," but as one who wishes to "join the disciples" (9:26). This is obviously a threatening circumstance for the community. How can it trust one who was only a short time before seeking to eradicate it? Was Paul's request simply a ruse to gain the names of others he could arrest? The real issue would seem to be whether or not to *flee* this man's presence, not whether to accept him as a fellow disciple. But that is what Paul wants, and his desire must be considered. Naturally enough, the group's instinct for self-preservation dominates at first: "They were all afraid of him, for they did not believe that he was a disciple" (9:26).

Barnabas now reenters the narrative of Acts. We saw him first as one who donated his possessions to the community and who received a new name from the apostles (4:36–37). He is a trusted member of the community. He takes Paul to the leaders and "narrates to them" (RSV "declared to them," 9:27) Paul's experiences: his vision, his dialogue with the risen Lord, his preaching in Damascus (9:27). The decision made by the apostles is not explicitly stated, but is clear from the sequel: Paul moves about freely, preaching in the name of Jesus (9:28); and when he meets opposition and the danger of death, the church rallies to help him and sends him safely to Tarsus (9:29–30).

The church's decision is remarkable enough: to accept as a fellow believer one who was actively persecuting the group is bold discernment. But even more stunning is the *basis* for the decision. It is not Paul's narration, but *Barnabas's* narrative of Paul's story which convinces the apostles. For Barnabas to do this, he first had to hear Paul's story and believe it. When he relates the events to the apostles, he does so not as a neutral reporter, but as one who has adopted Paul's own viewpoint: on the way, Paul saw the Lord (9:27). This narrative, we understand, had convincing power. It enabled the community to accept Paul as a fellow believer, because in the narrative they could discern the work of the Lord. There is no citation of Scripture here; only the narrative of experience. And it is a narrative mediated to the community for an outsider by one inside the church.

In these four passages, we have seen the church as church reaching decision. No set "form" characterizes all these accounts, but there are some consistent elements. One or the other may be missing, and what is central to one account may be peripheral to another. But we find in them the interaction of the assembly and its leaders in open fashion through public speech. We see a role for prayer by the assembly; for the narrative of experience; for interpreting Scripture in the light of that experience. In each passage, we also find situations which could have been understood in a purely negative fashion (the apostasy of an apostle, persecution, dissension, the approach of a foe) turned, by means of *narrative* and *interpretation*, into the basis for positive community decision. The correctness of the decisions is not always immediately clear. At the election of Matthias, the lots show divine approval; at the prayer for power, the Spirit makes its presence felt. But for the choosing of the seven, only subsequent experience validates the decision: when all but the apostles are scattered, they carry the message afield. In the case of Paul, the results remain ambiguous. His acceptance by the church immediately brings trouble upon it, and Paul stays on rather uneasy terms with the Jerusalem Church (cf. 15:1ff, 21:18–25).

These passages are not much more than thumbnail sketches. We can guess at the complexity of human motivation and circumstance beneath the surface. But the text shows nothing of the indecision, hesitancy, and conflict we suspect is always present when people try to make sense of their experience in the church. These decisions still bear the marks of inevitability. Only when we read the complete story of the conversion of Cornelius and the Jerusalem Council do we find a fully nuanced picture of the church reaching decision, where human frailty and the divine will are both impressively displayed.

From Cornelius to the Council: Stages of a Church Decision

The conversion of Cornelius created a crisis because he was a Gentile. The baptism of him and his household by Peter (Acts 10:48) anticipated a far more extensive mission to the Gentile world (14:27). Since before that conversion, the church, according to Luke, had been only Jewish, the innovation demanded a discernment both of the church and of this challenge. Was the conversion of the Gentiles legitimate? If so, on what grounds could they be considered part of God's people? It is not necessary to ask whether Cornelius was, in fact, the first Gentile convert, or whether

Peter really anticipated Paul (or the Hellenistic missionaries) in making this critical change. The point is that Luke shows us the process by which the church decided the issue, how it reached its decision.

The importance of the decision is shown by the placement of the account, and the close attention it receives. Acts 15 is the major turning point in the book of Acts. Before it, the Jerusalem mission dominates; after it, attention is almost exclusively focused on Paul's preaching all the way to Rome. The significance of the turning point can only be grasped, however, when Acts 15 is recognized as the climax to a story beginning in Acts 10. Nowhere else in Luke's writing do we find such painstaking attention to minute detail at each stage of the action. His narrative elsewhere moves lightly and rapidly. Here, it pauses, recapitulates, and reinterprets itself. The author does not want the reader to miss the meaning of these events.

The text's attention to human doubt and debate is all the more impressive, since Luke has shown the reader from the beginning of his writing that God intended the salvation of the Gentiles. The salvation brought by Jesus to Israel is a "light for revelation to the Gentiles" (Luke 2:32), and when John the Baptist precedes him in preaching, the Isaiah passage in Luke's version includes the words, "all flesh shall see the salvation of God" (Luke 3:6, cf. Isa. 40:5, LXX). The sending out of the seventy-(two) by Jesus in Luke 10:1–12 is often regarded as an anticipation of the Gentile mission, and may well be. After his resurrection, Jesus tells his witnesses that "forgiveness of sins should be preached in his name to all nations, beginning from Jerusalem" (Luke 24:47), and just before his ascension tells the eleven they will be his witnesses "to the end of the earth" (Acts 1:8). At Pentecost, Peter proclaims that the promise of the Holy Spirit is for those Jews who hear him and for "all that are far off, every one whom the Lord our God calls to him" (Acts 2:39). In a later speech, he declares that to the Jerusalemite Jews has Jesus been sent "first," suggesting that if they receive the prophet, the promise to Abraham will be fulfilled, for "in your posterity shall all the families of the earth be blessed" (Acts 3:25–26, cf. Gen. 22:18). We have also seen how the Holy Spirit directed the preaching to the Samaritans and the Ethiopian eunuch (Acts 8:4–40), though Luke may have regarded them as part of the restoration of Israel. In short, Luke has left his reader in no doubt concerning *God's* intention: from the beginning, God has willed the salvation of the Gentile world. The standpoint of the storyteller, which is shared with the reader, makes the event appear inevitable. It is the more striking, then, that Luke is so concerned to show the human process of coming to recognize and affirm God's intention.

To find the dynamics of decision making in this story, we must follow the plot sequentially. The process and the issues emerge slowly and in definite progression. Whether Gentiles can be preached to or even baptized is settled rather quickly. But the deeper *human* difficulty of fellowship between Jewish and Gentile believers is far harder to resolve. If both Jews and Gentiles are to be considered part of "God's people," will it be on even or uneven footing? On what basis will Gentiles be recognized and associated with? On the basis of their belief in the Messiah and the gift of the Holy Spirit, or on the basis of being circumcised and observing the law of Moses? Will the church split into two ethnically and ritually distinct bodies? Is Yahweh a tribal deity, or Lord of all? Will fellowship be determined by faith, or by precedent; by the experience of God, or by the rules of the community? At stake is the church's identity as witness to the work of God. Will the church decide to recognize and acknowledge actions of God which go beyond its present understanding, or will it demand that God work within its categories?

The Conversion: The First Decision (Acts 10:1–48)

[1]At Caesarea there was a man named Cornelius, a centurion of what was known as the Italian Cohort, [2]a devout man who feared God with all his household, gave alms liberally to the people, and prayed constantly to God. [3]About the ninth hour of the day he saw clearly in a vision an angel of God coming in and saying to him, "Cornelius." [4]And he stared at him in terror, and said, "What is it, Lord?" And he said to him, "Your prayers and your alms have ascended as a memorial before God. [5]And now send men to Joppa, and bring one Simon who is called Peter; [6]he is lodging with Simon, a tanner, whose house is by the seaside." [7]When the angel who spoke to him had departed, he called two of his servants and a devout soldier from among those that waited on him, [8]and having related everything to them, he sent them to Joppa.

[9]The next day, as they were on their journey and coming near the city, Peter went up on the housetop to pray, about the sixth hour. [10]And he became hungry and desired something to eat; but while they were preparing it, he fell into a trance [11]and saw the heaven opened, and something descending, like a great sheet, let down by four corners upon the earth. [12]In it were all kinds of animals and reptiles and birds of the air. [13]And there came a voice to him, "Rise, Peter; kill and eat." [14]But Peter said, "No, Lord; for I have never eaten anything

that is common or unclean." [15]And the voice came to him again a second time, "What God has cleansed, you must not call common." [16]This happened three times, and the thing was taken up at once to heaven.

[17]Now while Peter was inwardly perplexed as to what the vision he had seen might mean, behold, the men that were sent by Cornelius, having made inquiry for Simon's house, stood before the gate [18]and called out to ask whether Simon who was called Peter was lodging there. [19]And while Peter was pondering the vision, the Spirit said to him, "Behold, three men are looking for you. [20]Rise and go down, and accompany them without hesitation; for I have sent them." [21]And Peter went down to the men and said, "I am the one you are looking for; what is the reason for your coming?" [22]And they said, "Cornelius, a centurion, an upright and God-fearing man, who is well spoken of by the whole Jewish nation, was directed by a holy angel to send for you to come to his house, and to hear what you have to say." [23]So he called them in to be his guests.

The story begins with the religious experience of the Gentile Cornelius. He is not a member of God's people, but he is one who fears God and prays intensely (10:2). It is in prayer that he has the vision which begins this critical series of events. The vision of God's angel, whom Cornelius calls "Lord," is exceedingly short and to the point: "Send. . .and bring one Simon who is called Peter." Cornelius obeys the order without question or hesitation. He "narrates" all (RSV "related everything," 10:8) to his delegates, so they can adequately inform Peter. The intrusion of the Holy (see the "terror" of Cornelius in 10:4) and the divine direction are explicit here, but they require human trust and obedience to become effective.

Luke then shows us Simon Peter having a vision as well, while the men are on the road. He, too, is at prayer (10:9-16), but his vision is complex and confusing. He rejects the order to eat indiscriminately among clean and unclean food, on the basis of his previous experience and understanding as a pious Jew (10:14). He is not so quick as the Gentile Cornelius to heed the voice, even though the vision and its gnomic command, "What God has cleansed you must not call common," is repeated *three times* (10:15-16)!

Peter not only refuses the order but is thrown into utter confusion by his experience. Was it only a projection of his desires, since he was at the time so hungry (10:10)? Luke tells us that Peter was "inwardly perplexed as to what the vision he had seen might mean" (10:17). This confusion is emphasized in Acts 10:19. While Peter is "pondering the vision," the men arrive from Cornelius (10:17). The Spirit now gives Peter a definite nudge, telling him to go with them "without hesitation" The Greek of this phrase can also be translated "without discrimination" (10:20), and both senses are appropriate here. Peter listens to the men "narrate" what they had been told by Cornelius. We notice that now the message is slightly elaborated, including "to hear what you have to say" in 10:22. The narrative of Cornelius's experience by these men provides Peter with the first interpretation of his vision, and the basis for his first decision: "So he called them in to be his guests" (10:23). The "so" in this sentence is very definite in the Greek, indicating that Peter's response was to what he had heard from the men.

The importance of Peter's first response should be clear. Even though not fully *understanding* the direction of God given by the coincidence of vision and visit, he *obeys* it. Peter receives Gentiles into his abode as guests. He makes no discrimination. In this first scene, we see that the separate religious experience of two people—one inside the church, one outside of it—is mediated by narrative to form the basis for a common story. By believing the testimony of the messengers, Peter allows his own ambiguous experience to be interpreted. He is an individual believer discerning and deciding on behalf of God within the complexity and confusion of real life. Acts 10 continues.

   [23]The next day he rose and went off with them, and some of the brethren from Joppa accompanied him. [24]And on the following day they entered Caesarea. Cornelius was expecting them and had called together his kinsmen and close friends. [25]When Peter entered, Cornelius met him and fell down at his feet and worshiped him. [26]But Peter lifted him up, saying, "Stand up; I too am a man." [27]And as he talked with him, he went in and found many persons gathered; [28]and he said to them, "You yourselves know how unlawful it is for a Jew to associate with or visit any one of another nation; but God has shown me that I should not call any man common or unclean. [29]So when I was sent for, I came without objection. I ask then why you sent for me."
   [30]And Cornelius said, "Four days ago, about this hour, I was keeping the ninth hour of prayer in my house; and behold, a man stood before me in bright apparel, [31]saying, 'Cornelius, your prayer has been heard and your alms have been remembered before God. [32]Send therefore to Joppa and ask for Simon who is called Peter; he is lodging at the house of Simon, a tanner, by the seaside. [33]So I sent to you at once, and you have been kind enough to come. Now therefore we are all here present in the sight of God, to hear all that you have been commanded by the Lord."
   [34]And Peter opened his mouth and said: "Truly I perceive that God shows no partiality, [35]but in every nation any one who fears him and does what is right is acceptable to him."

The fact that some of Peter's Jewish Christian associates accompany him from Joppa to Caesarea (10:23) is of considerable importance for the rest of the story. They are also believers ("brethren"), and their presence raises Peter's act from the private to the communal level. They will witness the events still to follow. In the meantime, Cornelius also gathers associates (10:24). Something more than a private encounter is about to take place.

Peter has stopped questioning by Acts 10:27–28. He speaks with Cornelius and goes in with him to the larger gathering. This is another critical step for Peter. He has begun to see the implications of his vision, and he acts on them. He gives voice to his understanding in 10:28: "God has shown me that I should not call any man common or unclean." This is *not*, of course, literally what the voice from the vision had said. Only Peter's subsequent experience, shaped by Cornelius's narrative, has led him to this interpretation of the vision. He now understands the beasts as standing for peoples. The full meaning of "what God has cleansed" is still not clear to him. So Peter asks *Cornelius* to tell him more (10:29)!

Cornelius tells again, first-hand, the narrative of his religious experience (10:30–33). It contains still another interpretative addition concerning Peter's coming. Now he says that everyone is gathered in God's presence "to hear all that you have been commanded by the Lord"(10:33), a refinement of "to hear what you have to say" added by the men in 10:22. As a result of his meeting and conversation with Peter (10:27), Cornelius's expectation grows, as well as his own awareness of what his vision meant.

Peter responds to the narrative by stating in solemn fashion his own conclusion. He has now come to see what God had been trying to tell him all along. In Cornelius's story, mention was made of prayer and almsgiving, and Peter picks this up in his own statement: "In every nation any one who fears him and does what is right is acceptable to him"(10:34). The RSV translation, "doing right," misses the allusion. "Doing justice" is, in this tradition, equivalent to almsgiving, a work of mercy. And prayer is the acting out of "fear of God" (cf. 10:2). Peter's insight has radical significance. God has led him to see that it is not membership in a certain people which makes one acceptable to God, but the human response of "faith"—another way of saying "fear of God"—which is spelled out in mercy. And this is found among all peoples.

Peter also sees that this acceptance by God is not accidental or arbitrary, but is rooted in God's nature. There is "no respecting of persons" with

God. In the language of this tradition, the phrase refers to the sort of prejudice or partiality judges might show when given bribes (cf. Lev. 19:15). God is not that sort of judge. God's righteousness is not swayed by considerations of ethnic origin or religious affiliation. Peter now realizes that God is God of the Gentiles as well as of the Jews. The God worshiped in the church is not a tribal deity (cf. also Rom.2:11; 3:29-30). Peter also sees the implications. If the Gentiles are acceptable to *God*, then they ought to be acceptable to the *church*, which claims to witness to God. On this basis, he makes the decision to preach the gospel to Cornelius and his household.

[36]"You know the word which he sent to Israel, preaching good news of peace by Jesus Christ (he is Lord of all), [37]the word which was proclaimed throughout all Judea, beginning from Galilee after the baptism which John preached: [38]how God anointed Jesus of Nazareth with the Holy Spirit and with power; how he went about doing good and healing all that were oppressed by the devil, for God was with him. [39]And we are witnesses to all that he did both in the country of the Jews and in Jerusalem. They put him to death by hanging him on a tree; [40]but God raised him on the third day and made him manifest; [41]not to all the people but to us who were chosen by God as witnesses, who ate and drank with him after he rose from the dead. [42]And he commanded us to preach to the people, and testify that he is the one ordained by God to be judge of the living and the dead. [43]To him all the prophets bear witness that everyone who believes in him receives forgiveness of sins through his name."
[44]While Peter was still saying this, the Holy Spirit fell on all who heard the word. [45]And the believers from among the circumcised who came with Peter were amazed, because the gift of the Holy Spirit had been poured out even on the Gentiles. [46]For they heard them speaking in tongues and extolling God. Then Peter declared, [47]"Can any one forbid water for baptizing these people who have received the Holy Spirit just as we have?" [48]And he commanded them to be baptized in the name of Jesus Christ. Then they asked him to remain for some days.

Peter's message for the household of Cornelius is itself a *narrative* of the events to which he and his fellows are witnesses (10:39, 41). Peter's story begins where the gospel does, with the "word which he sent to Israel" through Jesus' preaching of peace (10:36), and ends with the realization he had just had in a deeper fashion than before, "every one who believes in him receives forgiveness of sins through his name" (10:43). Remembering the story enables it to move forward. The statement that this gift is available to his Gentile listeners precipitates a new religious experience among them. While they are still listening, the Holy Spirit falls on them (10:44).

The reaction of the onlookers is expecially interesting. We remember that they are *Jewish* believers who had accompanied Peter from Joppa (10:23). They are more than passive witnesses. They are the ones who identify the event's meaning. They hear people speaking in tongues and praising God, and *therefore* conclude that the Holy Spirit had been given to the Gentiles as well (Acts 10:45–46). From the effect, they deduce the cause. How? Because they themselves had first experienced the Spirit in such a fashion. Because they know from their own story that the Holy Spirit gifted them with ecstasy and praise (Acts 2:1–4), they could recognize the same gift here. Peter's question to them presupposes such a shared recognition. The Gentiles have received the Holy Spirit ''just as we have'' (10:47). No words of the prophets nor Law interpret this event, but the previous religious experience of the witnesses. It was this which enabled them to discern the movement of God's Spirit in the present. On the basis of this recognition, Peter orders the people to be baptized (10:48). He has come to a still deeper understanding of his initial vision. Those he had previously thought unclean have been gifted by God's Spirit in the same way he had. This awareness has resulted from his own experience, the narrative of others' experience, and his witnessing the religious experience of others. From this, he has come to recognize God at work, and has the Gentiles baptized. Peter's decision is for God. The ritual acceptance into the church follows the perception that God had already accepted them into his people.

Peter in Jerusalem: The Decision Defended (Acts 11:1–18)

[1]Now the apostles and the brethren who were in Judea heard that the Gentiles also had received the word of God. [2]So when Peter went up to Jerusalem, the circumcision party criticized him, [3]saying, ''Why did you go to uncircumcised men and eat with them?'' [4]But Peter began and explained to them in order: [5]''I was in the city of Joppa praying; and in a trance I saw a vision, something descending, like a great sheet, let down from heaven by four corners; and it came down to me. [6]Looking at it closely I observed animals and beasts of prey and reptiles and birds of the air. [7]And I heard a voice saying to me, 'Rise, Peter; kill and eat.' [8]But I said, 'No, Lord; for nothing common or unclean has ever entered my mouth.' [9]But the voice answered a second time from heaven, 'What God has cleansed you must not call common.' [10]This happened three times, and all was drawn up again into heaven. [11]At that very

moment three men arrived at the house in which we were, sent to me from Caesarea. ¹²And the Spirit told me to go with them, making no distinction. These six brethren also accompanied me, and we entered the man's house. ¹³And he told us how he had seen the angel standing in his house and saying, 'Send to Joppa and bring Simon called Peter; ¹⁴He will declare to you a message by which you will be saved, you and all your household.' ¹⁵As I began to speak, the Holy Spirit fell on them just as on us at the beginning. ¹⁶And I remembered the word of the Lord, how he said, 'John baptized with water, but you shall be baptized with the Holy Spirit.' ¹⁷If then God gave the same gift to them as he gave to us when we believed in the Lord Jesus Christ, who was I that I could withstand God?'' ¹⁸When they heard this they were silenced. And they glorified God, saying, ''Then to the Gentiles also God has granted repentance unto life.''

This is an altogether astonishing passage. Precisely its apparent redundancy within the larger plot forces us to recognize the significance of the previous event and the need for it to be ratified. Here we see Peter's individual decision challenged by certain members of his home community (11:3), and then affirmed by the community as a whole (11:18). We learn from this that *opposition*, openly expressed, is part of the decision-making process. It enables discernment to take place, by exposing the options to full view. It is part of the testing of the Spirit. When the church argues over its actions, then it discovers the roots of its implicit understanding which gave rise to the action, and can begin to articulate its faith in a more explicit way. We see that the issue of relations with Gentiles in the church is now reaching the level of church discussion and discernment, properly speaking.

It is perhaps natural that ''those from the circumcision party'' should criticize Peter (11:2). Their attack, however, is not directed to his baptizing the Gentiles, but returns to the level of Peter's first understanding. They attack his having *eaten* with Gentiles (11:3), that is, having fellowship with them. The issue of communion is explicitly raised. Just because Gentiles have ''received the word of God,'' which is acknowledged in 11:1, does not mean that they should have full communion with Jewish believers, or be considered as members of God's people in the fullest sense. The problem is real. For a Jew to eat without attending to ritual purity meant to lose his or her Jewish identity. Part of ritual purity, however, means not ''giving dogs what is holy'' (Matt.7:6). How can meals be both sacred, yet shared with unclean people? His opponents imply that Peter has, by eating with

Gentiles, himself gone against his identity as one of God's people, and has, furthermore, jeopardized the identity of the community.

To answer the challenge, Peter is required to show the deeper implications of the Gentiles' conversion. The Gentile believers, he says, received the *same gift* as did the Jewish believers in the beginning (11:15). Thus the pertinence of Peter taking along his associates. Peter stresses that he took along "these six brethren" and that "we" entered the house (11:12). There is more than a rhetorical ploy to this statement. Peter is calling his associates to witness—as Jews—to the accuracy of his narrative. More than that, they must stand on their own experience, for they were involved from the start, and had been, in fact, the ones who had certified that the Gentiles were receiving the Holy Spirit. If these six brethren now dispute Peter's account on other grounds, they run the risk of denying their own experience of God's power.

Of greater importance for our investigation of the decision-making process is the *way* in which Peter responds. When challenged, he does not stand on his authority as an apostle, or argue from the Scripture, for neither really covers the situation. He neither argues nor asserts. Rather, *he narrates his own experience*. This and this alone moves the others to accept and ratify his decision. Peter tells them, in effect, that from the first vision on, he was led to understand that God was at work in these events. Thus we feel the force of his final question, framed as a simple conditional, "If then God gave the same gift to them . . . who was I that I could withstand God?" (11:17). Peter states it neatly. The refusal to recognize the clear evidence of God's action is to oppose God.

Two further aspects of the passage deserve some attention. First, Peter narrates these events "in order" (11:4). This is the same term used by Luke in the prologue to the Gospel (Luke 1:3), and has considerable significance. By telling the gospel story "in order," Luke wishes to give his reader "security" or "certainty." So here, by telling his tale "in order," Peter's narrative, we understand, has a convincing quality. The narrative itself is the vehicle of persuasion.

The second aspect of Peter's story is even more intriguing. We find two major additions to the story this time around. In 11:14, Cornelius's vision is given its final elaboration: he can expect from Peter a message "by which you will be saved." The past is *shaped* by the realization granted by the present. Another and even more exciting addition is found in 11:16, where

Peter says he remembered the word of the Lord when he saw the Holy Spirit fall on the Gentiles. The experience of the present *selects* what is remembered from the past. This outpouring of the Spirit stimulates Peter's recall of Jesus' words on the Spirit. In Luke-Acts, however, the saying he remembers is not one of the earthly but of the resurrected Lord. He told it to those waiting for the baptism of the Holy Spirit at Pentecost (Acts 1:5). That was, however, a small band of *Jewish* disciples. When Peter sees these Gentiles receive the Holy Spirit, he remembers Jesus' words, but with an entirely new application. What Jesus said to Jews is seen to apply to Gentiles as well. The words of Jesus are given new understanding because of the continuing work of the Spirit. The experience of God's activity in the present acts as a key for the interpretation of the Scripture, and now, we see, for the sayings of Jesus as well.

The Jerusalem community recognizes that the Gentiles have "been given the gift of repentance unto life," but the issue of relations has not been solved. The implications of God's will and Peter's decision have not yet been articulated by the church as a whole. The question whether Gentiles must become Jewish before they can be part of the people of God still remains. And if they do not, how can Jewish believers associate with them, and still be faithful to God's revelation?

The Jerusalem Council: The Decision Opposed and Affirmed (Acts 14:26—15:35)

After the confrontation between Peter and the Judean brethren, and before the Apostolic Council, Luke shows how the preaching to the Gentiles became more than a singular and private decision. He tells how "Greeks" were evangelized in Antioch (11:19–26), and how the missionary journey of Paul and Barnabas became, in Antioch of Pisidia, a mission to the Gentiles as well (13:46–48). In contrast to the Cornelius episode, these steps are not accompanied by agonizing deliberation, but appear to be directed by God through circumstances. The work is certified in the first instance by the sending of Barnabas to Antioch from Jerusalem (11:22), and in the second by the signs and wonders which God worked through Paul and Barnabas among the Gentiles (15:12). The Gentiles are becoming Christians now in many places. More than a purely local decision, therefore, is required on the issues already raised concerning conversion and communion. The narrative shows us next how these questions get raised to the level of a conscious church decision, and shows us how the process of reaching decision is a theological process.

> [26]And from there they sailed to Antioch, where they had been commended to the grace of God for the work which they had fulfilled. [27]And when they arrived, they gathered the church together and declared all that God had done with them, and how he had opened a door of faith to the Gentiles. [28]And they remained no little time with disciples. [Acts 15 follows.]
> [1]But some men came down from Judea and were teaching the brethren, "Unless you are circumcised according to the custom of Moses, you cannot be saved." [2]And when Paul and Barnabas had no small dissension and debate with them, Paul and Barnabas and some of the others were appointed to go up to Jerusalem to the apostles and the elders about this question. [3]So, being sent on their way by the church, they passed through both Phoenicia and Samaria, reporting the conversion of the Gentiles, and they gave great joy to all the brethren.

A conflict in the Church of Antioch makes the Jerusalem Council necessary. The Antioch controversy is generated by the return of Paul and Barnabas from their first missionary trip. They gather the church and narrate what God had done through them, how he had "opened a door of faith for the Gentiles" (14:27; cf. 13:48). The Church of Antioch is next visited by another party, "some men from Judea" (15:1). We remember that Paul and Barnabas *belong* to this community; they were sent out by it (13:1-3) and have fulfilled its mission (14:26). These other men are interlopers. And that makes their charge all the more insidious. They say, "*You* cannot be saved . . ."(15:1). They are saying this to the brothers, that is, the believers at Antioch. They are not only challenging the mission of Paul and Barnabas, but the integrity of the Antiochean Church itself, which, it appears, consisted at least in part of Gentiles (cf. 11:20). We remember now that this church had already been approved by Jerusalem by the sending of Barnabas to it (11:22). By challenging the Antioch community at the level of its own salvation, the Judeans put the question in its starkest terms: is the grace of God and the gift of the Holy Spirit sufficient for salvation, or not? And this touches another question: is God's work going to be acknowledged as it manifests itself, or only as it conforms to the church's presuppositions?

The narrative shows no embarrassment at this opposition, or the intensity of the debate it generates. There was "no small dissension and debate" (15:2). Luke uses phrases like these for emphasis (cf. 14:28), and so indicates a great turmoil. Here, as with Peter before the Judean brethren (11:3), open opposition is part of the discernment process.

The assembly in Antioch is active throughout. They are gathered to hear the narrative of Paul and Barnabas, and after the dispute "they" send representatives to Jerusalem (15:2). The Greek does not make it clear whom they send. The "some of the others" could refer back to the opponents. In this case, the church would have sent as a delegation both parties to the dispute. It is more likely, however, that those who were sent off share the views of Barnabas and Paul, for as they travel they "narrate" to other churches "the conversion of the Gentiles," and stir up enthusiasm for this initiative (15:3).

The sending of a delegation from Antioch indicates the willingness of the daughter church to hear the judgment of the apostles and elders in Jerusalem on this issue (15:2). At the same time, it is something of a confrontation. Jerusalem had once approved this community, but now those who came from Judea were disturbing it. Was Jerusalem going back on its word and breaking fellowship? The representatives from Antioch have witnessed God at work among them, and in the mission carried out by Paul and Barnabas. This difficulty was created not by internal dissension, but by attack from the outside. The Antiochean group is therefore going to the source of the trouble, to call the Jerusalem Church to account. This is a matter, after all, which affects the integrity of the Antiochean Church's existence as "Christian."

So casual is the mention of Paul and Barnabas narrating their experiences to the churches in Phoenicia and Samaria that one can almost miss it and its significance. It shows us again the power of narrative to convince. But it also shows us how the issue raised in Antioch is of concern to other communities. This is no longer just a local dispute, but a challenge which must be decided by the church as such.

> 4When they came to Jerusalem, they were welcomed by the church and the apostles and the elders, and they declared all that God had done with them. 5But some believers who belonged to the party of the Pharisees rose up, and said, "It is necessary to circumcise them, and to charge them to keep the law of Moses."

The whole Church of Jerusalem, with its leaders, greets the delegation from Antioch. The assembly as such is given the chance to hear both sides of the debate, for the ultimate discernment and decision rests with it. The conflict is stated sharply. The party from Antioch ''narrates'' once more ''all that God had done with them.'' Their position is communicated best by the recountal of their experience of God's work.

The Pharisaic party, on the other hand, argues on the basis of theological principle and precedent. Their ''it is necessary,'' we assume, rests on those warrants. Because of the way this story finally ends, it is easy to dismiss these ''legalists'' and their position. For us to appreciate the decision that was made, however, it is important to recognize the force of their position. It was theologically respectable. If part of God's revelation consisted in the practice of circumcision as the symbol of entrance into the people (and it did); and if all the previous revelation by God had taught the necessity of keeping the Law to be a full part of the people and receive its blessing (as it surely did); then their statement is neither superficial nor silly. In fact, the weight of the evidence would seem to be on their side.

The only thing which could counter such powerful precedent is the conviction that the God who revealed in the past was active in these events now, and that God's way of maintaining continuity in revelation may not be the same as ours. This, then, becomes the issue for the church's discernment. Will it fall back on its deeply rooted (and revealed!) perceptions of how God ''ought'' to act, or will it recognize that God moves ahead of its perceptions? Perhaps an anticipation of the outcome can be seen in the very reception of the delegation from Antioch. As Peter with Cornelius, the act of hospitality is already a kind of recognition.

> [6]The apostles and elders were gathered together to consider this matter. [7]And after there had been much debate, Peter rose and said to them, ''Brethren, you know that in the early days God made choice among you, that by my mouth the Gentiles should hear the word of the gospel and believe. [8]And God who knows the heart bore witness to them, giving them the Holy Spirit just as he did to us; [9]and he made no distinction between us and them, but cleansed their hearts by faith. [10]Now therefore why do you make trial of God by putting a yoke upon the neck of the disciples which neither our fathers nor we have been able to bear? [11]But we believe that we shall be saved through the grace of the Lord Jesus, just as they will.''
> [12]And all the assembly kept silence; and they listened to Barnabas and Paul as they related what signs and wonders God had done through them among the Gentiles.

After the public statement of positions, it appears that the matter is left for the debate of the apostles and elders who gather together (15:6). The larger assembly is still present and the discussion takes place before them (cf. 15:12, 22), but the leaders now actively articulate the question. After that initial sharp clash of views, there follows a great debate (15:7). For a writer of marked irenic tendencies, Luke exposes much conflict in this narrative.

Peter's testimony dominates this section. As when he was before the elders in Jerusalem, he prefaces his final question, "Why do you make trial of God?" with the narrative of his experience. It is, we see, really the narrative of both his and Cornelius's experience, now fully become one story. This is the third telling of the Cornelius episode. It is now reduced to its essentials. The whole sequence is viewed from the ending, and Peter's insight has matured. He no longer elaborates the puzzlement and confusion, but speaks confidently of the story as one told by God. *God* is the subject of every verb in this account. God chose, testified, did not discriminate, and cleansed the hearts of the Gentiles by faith (15:7–9).

At last, the full meaning of the vision is clear. Peter was not to discriminate between people (10:20) because God does not discriminate, being "no respecter of persons" (10:34; RSV "shows no partiality"). The clean and unclean of the vision are seen now in this light: "God cleansed their hearts by faith." That in fact God did so cleanse their hearts was certified by the gift of the Holy Spirit to the Gentiles, "just as he did to us" (15:8, cf. 11:15). This is what Peter means by God's witnessing. The question he puts to the opponents is therefore a direct challenge. He had earlier regarded any hesitation to baptize with water those God had given the Spirit as a "preventing" of God (RSV "withstand," 11:17). Now he calls the attempt to impose conditions on the gift of grace to the Gentiles a "testing" of God (RSV "make trial of God," 15:10). Within this tradition, Peter's phrasing suggests an active rebellion against God (cf. Exod. 15:25; 17:2; Ps.77:46, LXX). Peter's interpretative narrative of his experience places the issue on properly theological grounds. Can one recognize God's work in the world? *Yes.* And once the recognition is made, the church's decision should follow.

Peter reminds his listeners that what he is saying is something they already know. He appeals to *their* previous experience and understanding: "You know" (Acts 15:7); "Just as he did to us" (15:8); "We believe" (15:11). This last turn is stunning. Peter states the theological truth he has learned from his experience as a *shared* belief! The content of this statement is also unexpected. We could anticipate his saying that Gentiles are saved on the same basis as Jews—that would be enough. But his statement reverses the situation. He says that Jewish believers will be saved by the grace of the Lord Jesus, *just as the Gentiles* (15:11). The implication of this reversal is that Peter has come to learn from his experience of God's work among the Gentiles the basis for his *own* salvation. If those who did not keep the Law were saved by grace, then that must be the basis of his being saved, who had only with difficulty borne the Law. Can it be that Peter and the Jewish Christians needed the conversion of Cornelius more than Cornelius did?

Peter's testimony clears the way for Barnabas and Paul. The assembly listens in silence as they "narrate" all the signs and wonders God had worked through them among the Gentiles (15:12). "Signs and wonders" are the consistent Lukan signal for the way God validates human ministry, from Moses to Paul (cf. Acts 2:19, 22, 43; 5:12; 6:8; 7:36; 14:3). Now Paul and Barnabas, from the perspective of the present, can view the tumultuous and ambiguous events of that journey as *God's* work, just as Peter could with hindsight speak of his story as one told by God. But just as important, they spoke of God doing these things "through them." They recount their *own* experience of God's activity. The narrative is their only argument. Now it has been joined by Peter's story, so that the narratives of these three missionaries together present a single story for the church's discernment. Although all are apostles, they appear here not as arbiters but as witnesses, speaking in their own voice of God's work in them.

> [13]After they finished speaking, James replied, "Brethren, listen to me. [14]Simeon has related how God first visited the Gentiles, to take out of them a people for his name. [15]And with this the words of the prophets agree, as it is written,
>> [16]'After this I will return,
>> and I will rebuild the dwelling of
>>   David, which has fallen;
>> I will rebuild its ruins,
>> and I will set it up,
>> [17]that the rest of men may seek the
>>   Lord,
>> and all the Gentiles who are called
>>   by my name,
>> [18]says the Lord, who has made these
>>   things known from of old.'

[19]Therefore my judgment is that we should not trouble those of the Gentiles who turn to God, [20]but should write to them to abstain from the pollutions of idols and from unchastity and from what is strangled and from blood. [21]For from early generations Moses has had in every city those who preach him, for he is read every sabbath in the synagogues.''

We need not ask why James's determination is decisive (for it surely is), but should look at the shape of his decision and his reasons for making it. He makes a solemn judgment (15:19), though one which requires the approval of the assembly (15:22, 25). As the spokesperson of the Jerusalem Church, from which the trouble started, he clearly accepts the basic position of the delegates from Antioch. He considers it wrong to ''trouble'' the Gentile converts any longer. There is at least an implied acknowledgment that they *had* been troubled by the Judean party. The fundamental freedom of the Gentile believers (and therefore of God!) is affirmed.

James next deals with the grounds for fellowship. The position of the Christians from the Pharisaic party, that circumcision and the keeping of all of Torah was necessary, is completely rejected. But James thinks that some observances are appropriate. It is important to see why. The first two stipulations—turning away from idolatry and sexual immorality— are axiomatic for Gentile converts as well as Jewish believers (cf., e.g., 1 Thess. 1:9–10, 4:3–8). The biggest concession to Jewish believers is the requirement to abstain from ''what is strangled and from blood.'' Why is this required of Gentiles? This is the sort of regulation that comes into play precisely in the context of *eating together*, that is, fellowship. And it is intended to enable those who are sincere keepers of the Law to engage in such fellowship with Gentiles. Rather than limit the possibility of fellowship with Gentiles, this requirement opens it, by freeing the conscience of Torah-keeping Christians. James considers these observances reasonable because they would not appear to those who were God-fearers as new obligations at all. So pervasive had been the influence of the Law of Moses in the Diaspora because of the network of synagogues, that even Gentiles would be familiar with these norms (15:21). James decides for the action of God among the Gentiles and resoundingly affirms their freedom and fellowship within the people.

James gives two reasons for his decision: the narrative of Simeon/Peter (15:14) and the interpretation of the Scripture (15:15–18). James more than alludes to Peter's story; he makes it his own by adopting Peter's characterizations of the events. He also gives it another level of interpretation. Now

the Cornelius episode is seen as the first *visitation* of God to the Gentiles.
God's visiting marks an intervention for salvation (cf. Luke 1:68, 78; 7:16;
19:44; Acts 7:23; Exod. 3:16; 4:31, LXX). And by bringing them salvation, God has shaped from among them "a people for his name": the Gentiles are to be regarded as fully part of God's people (cf. Luke 1:17, 68,
77; 2:32; 7:16; 24:19; Acts 3:23; 4:10; 5:12). James recognizes in Peter's
story the work of God.

More than that, Peter's story is the key to understanding the Scripture.
James's way of introducing the citation is at first puzzling, then illumina-
ting. He does not say, "This agrees with the prophets," but, "The words
of the prophets agree with *this*," and the reference is to the story Peter
has just told: how God was at work in these events. James then cites Amos
9:11–12 from the Greek translation (LXX), in which the Hebrew, "That
they may possess the remnant of Edom," comes out as, "That the rest of
men may seek the Lord." James sees that the Gentiles are also "called
by my name," and that their conversion means the rebuilding of "the
dwelling of David, which has fallen" (15:16). The restored people of God
embraces both Gentiles and Jews. What is remarkable, however, is that
the text is confirmed by the narrative, not the narrative by the Scripture.
As Peter had come to a new understanding of Jesus' words because of the
gift of the Spirit, so here the Old Testament is illuminated and interpreted
by the narrative of God's activity in the present. On the basis of the narrative and of the Scripture, therefore, James decides for God rather than
for precedent.

[22]Then it seemed good to the apostles and the elders, with the whole church,
to choose men from among them and send them to Antioch with Paul and
Barnabas. They sent Judas called Barsabbas, and Silas, leading men among
the brethren, [23]with the following letter: "The brethren, both the apostles and
the elders, to the brethren who are of the Gentiles in Antioch and Syria and
Cilicia, greeting. [24]Since we have heard that some persons from us have troubled you with words, unsettling your minds, although we gave them no instructions, [25]it has seemed good to us, having come to one accord, to choose men
and send them to you with our beloved Barnabas and Paul, [26]men who have
risked their lives for the sake of our Lord Jesus Christ. [27]We have therefore
sent Judas and Silas, who themselves will tell you the same things by word
of mouth. [28]For it has seemed good to the Holy Spirit and to us to lay upon
you no greater burden than these necessary things: [29]that you abstain from
what has been sacrificed to idols and from blood and from what is strangled
and from unchastity. If you keep yourselves from these, you will do well.
Farewell."

The decision articulated by James is approved by the leaders and the
whole assembly; they "come to one accord" (15:25). Even the determination of James required discernment and decision by the whole assembly
(15:22). The group makes two practical decisions. It will send a letter to
Antioch, and with it a personal delegation (15:22–23). Because Paul and
Barnabas are highly praised (15:25) and because the Jerusalem delegation
is made up of "leading men" who are to confirm the decision (15:22),
this letter becomes more than a decree from on high. It becomes an act
of fellowship between churches. The gesture is accented by the language
of the letter itself.

Although the Jerusalem Church denies responsibility for the activity of
the troublemakers, it grants that they came "from us." and, by acknowl-
edging that they had unsettled the minds of the believers at Antioch effectively apologizes for the harm they did. The statement "it has seemed good
to the Holy Spirit and to us" is more than rhetoric. The decision reached
by the church has resulted from the discernment of the Spirit. This church
is able to agree with Peter that the Gentiles had received the Holy Spirit
"just like us," because it was a church open to the work of that Spirit and
able to recognize it in the narrations of others.

30So when they were sent off, they went down to Antioch; and having
gathered the congregation together, they delivered the letter. 31And when they
read it, they rejoiced at the exhortation. 32And Judas and Silas, who were
themselves prophets, exhorted the brethren with many words and strengthened
them. 33And after they had spent some time, they were sent off in peace by
the brethren to those who had sent them. 35But Paul and Barnabas remained
in Antioch, teaching and preaching the word of the Lord, with many others
also.

These decisions have been made by the communities as such. The sending of a delegation from Antioch in the first place was a church decision; so
was the reception of it by the Jerusalem Church. The community, in turn,
sent back a delegation with the letter. They are now greeted by this whole
congregation. The Jerusalem community fulfills its mission by exhorting
and strengthening the brethren in Antioch. They do not simply drop off the
letter. The delegates ensure, by their long stay with the church at Antioch
(15:33), by their standing in the Jerusalem Church (15:22), and by their
being prophets (15:31), that this community is fully recognized as being in
communion with the Jerusalem Church. The Jerusalem community shows
great pastoral concern for those whom, wittingly or not, it has harmed.

It works strenuously to renew fellowship. And as a consequence of these multiple gestures, the Jerusalem delegates are sent back home "in peace" (15:33). So, we understand, there is peace among God's churches.

Decision Making as a Theological Process

In the story of Cornelius's conversion and the Apostolic Council, we see the early church deciding its future in a fundamental way. It determines how it understands *itself* as God's people, and how it understands *God* who calls it as a people. The process is theological. First, it is an articulation of *faith* seeking understanding, not in some abstract sense, but in an immediate and practical way: how can we understand the actions of God which go beyond our previous grasp of the way God acts? Second, it is the faith of the *church* which is articulated. The story begins with the experience of two individuals, and expands step-by-step into a debate and decision of the church as a whole. In the process, the church discovers new dimensions of what "we believe" (15:11). Third, it is the church's faith in *God* which is articulated. The basic decision, after all, is to let God be God, to say "yes" to the work of the Lord which goes before the church's ability to understand or even perceive it.

The decision is not made all at once. It is not made by the entire church from the beginning. It is not made on the basis of a priori principles and practices. Even the Scripture and the words of Jesus are reread. The decision, rather, is the result of *a long process*, involving many believers in many places, and the decisions of many local communities. The experiences of diverse people and the narrative of those experiences—in an ever widening circle—provide the primary theological data. As those who testify speak of their experience of God, so do those who listen weigh what is said: they exercise discernment. The people who have these experiences, moreover, are people already attentive to the Lord in prayer, and thus open to the new and surprising ways God might act, both in their own and others' lives. Slowly, the story of individuals becomes the narrative of the church.

We see how the stories of Cornelius and Peter interpret each other; how Peter's progressive insight into his vision depends on Cornelius's narrative. We hear Peter telling the tale "in order" before the elders in Jerusalem (11:4), convincing them of the rightness of his decision. We see how the narratives of Peter, Paul, and Barnabas in turn provide the basis for the decision of the church at the Council. The church, in short, is able to discern what God is doing because it is silent and listens to the story of what God is doing in others. Without these narratives, the church cannot discern, and therefore it cannot decide in a theologically responsible way.

In the four earlier accounts of decision making, we saw how narrative and scriptural interpretation were intertwined. In this final account, we have seen two remarkable instances of the same thing. Peter is given new understanding of the words of Jesus because of the new gift of the Holy Spirit. And James reads the prophet Amos with new meaning because of the story of Peter. The words of Jesus and the Scripture are normative for the believers, but in a way which allows new and deeper understanding. Throughout these accounts, the experience of God's activity stimulates the church to reread the Scripture and to discover ever new ways in which God maintains continuity with himself.

Other aspects of the decision-making process in these passages deserve attention: the active role of the assembly and not just leaders; the importance of silence and prayer for discernment to take place; the necessity of opposition and debate openly carried out; the significance of personal and pastoral communication of decisions once made. But I have deliberately concentrated on those components which make the process of reaching decision in the church a theological process: the experience of God, the narrative of that experience, its discernment, and the interpretation of the Word of God.

I emphasize that these elements of theological decision making are found in the narrative of Luke-Acts, and only *as* narrative. It is possible, I suggest, to read this text in its literary integrity as a vehicle for theological reflection in the church. As such, it can stand as a witness to the church in every age, asking it to consider whether and in what manner its own processes of decision making are articulations of faith in God.

4

DISCERNMENT

No component of the decision-making process found in the New Testament writings is more alien to our own, and therefore more in need of attention, than *discernment*. The Spirit-filled church is required to test the Spirit. Why do so many of us regard that as a strange and threatening proposition? Perhaps because it demands of the church explicit recognition that it is more than an ethical society. Perhaps also because it demands of the members the sort of faithful obedience which is not automatically validated externally by prescriptions or precedents. Discernment requires commitment and risk.

A more legitimate worry, however, keeps some of us from enthusiastically embracing discernment even as a concept. This is the way it has been used in practice. Particularly in churches with strong spiritual urges, discernment has been used as a tool of spiritual manipulation. Charges of "false prophecy" cover for personality and power conflicts within the group. Since some are considered to have more "power of discernment" than others, they are in a position to judge whether others "have" the Spirit. This is dangerous stuff, and rightly to be avoided. Not even Paul, who soberly claimed to have the "Spirit of God" (1 Cor. 7:40), presumed to judge the consciences of others, or decide whether some marriages were "in the Lord"—a decision later charismatic leaders would not hesitate to make. The excesses of spiritual totalitarians, however, should not make the church abandon this most precious spiritual gift.

The first legitimate use of discernment is in one's own search for God's will in the response of faith. Each is responsible for this, and no one can take over this responsibility from another (cf. Rom. 14:4, Matt. 7:3-15). The community as a whole, however, is expected to exercise discernment in matters which affect it as a whole. All discern the words of prophecy spoken in the assembly (1 Cor. 14:29), expel the rebellious deviant (1 Cor. 5:3-5; Matt. 18:15-20), decide matters of leadership (Acts 6:1-6) and fellowship (Acts 10:1—15: 35). The community does not judge the salvation of others; that is God's business. But the church must look to its integrity as a witness to God, and therefore exercise discernment concerning the movement of the Spirit within it. But how is the work of the Spirit made available for discernment?

That question leads to another difficulty with discernment, namely, the idea that it has to do with the behavior of others, as though the community could judge a person's state before God. Only when extreme deviant behavior has tested the church's tolerance to the breaking point does the community expel a member, and then only to maintain the integrity of its own identity (cf. 1 Cor. 5:1-5). The ritual of excommunication expresses outwardly a spiritual alienation which has already taken place, not between the member and God, but between the member and the *group*. Discernment, however, should not be evaluated on the basis of these extreme situations. In the ordinary life of the church, discernment does not have to do with the behavior of the members. It deals, rather, with the *speech* of others which tries to express God's activity inside and outside the visible community. But what kind of speech makes itself available for such discernment?

I have asked two questions which may have the same answer: the narrative of experience. This kind of speech can give voice to the movement of the Spirit within the assembly as a whole, and it can reveal the spiritual attitudes and orientations which motivate behavior within the church. We have seen in the Acts account how multiple individual narratives enabled a community narrative to develop. As that happened, the church was able to exercise discernment concerning the work of the Spirit within it, and decide for God. The narrative of experience is the prerequisite for the kind of discernment required for the church to reach decision as an articulation of faith.

Such narratives are important for all decisions made by the church as community of faith. Decisions on buildings and maintenance may appear banal, but can require of a community an examination of itself and its witness. Choosing between new hymnals and a new heating system may test the church's values in a powerfully searching way. The way the members express, by narrative, their experience of God in this church will enable the community to discern which of these choices best articulates its faith. A church which must choose between an aesthetic heritage and the opportunity to make millions for missionary efforts, if it will allow a skyscraper to be built over its head, has a splendid chance to articulate its faith in the reaching of that decision, by hearing the narrative of its members' experience of God in that place, and its meaning. And precisely because the situation and story of each church is different, it *cannot* avoid the responsibility of discernment in these decisions.

Decisions concerning the church's involvement in social and political movements, or issues of public morality, challenge both the community's understanding of itself and the gospel it seeks to proclaim. They force it to ask "What is our gospel," and in the process, they will read the Scripture with new urgency, impelled by the narratives of experience of those within the church and those outside it.

Three Cases for Discernment

Decisions on membership and fellowship raise "identity" issues in a direct way, and call even more urgently for the sort of narratives which will help the church discern the call of God for the present. There are at least three such issues facing local churches and worldwide communions today. They have in various ways been debated at higher levels. But because they have not been decided theologically at the local level, they remain alive and troublesome.

I discuss these issues not because they are the only or even the most important questions facing the church today, but for three reasons I hope are appropriate: a) to my mind, they are addressed particularly well by the Scripture passages analyzed in this book; b) they are all issues of sharp relevance to my own Catholic tradition; and c) I have personal knowledge of all three from my life and my work as a seminary teacher. By no means are the issues themselves restricted to the Catholic tradition. The issue of women priests is especially sharp for Catholics now, but it was so for Episcopalians only yesterday; and the wider issue of effective, not merely token, leadership by women—both ordained and lay—is critical for all churches. The question of fellowship with the divorced and remarried is an explicit, even legal, problem for Catholics. But it is equally if less formally a difficulty for many other Christian communities, especially those with a more conservative tradition. And the crisis of conscience posed by homosexuality in the church must be faced by all Christians.

I will not, of course, solve these issues here, or even adequately present them. They are complex and difficult. That is why I want to comment on elements that I think have been absent in the process of making these decisions until now.

The Leadership of Women in the Church

To some extent, this is an issue for all churches. Although many Protestant denominations have ordained women for years, there is still some resistance to full leadership—both ordained and lay—by women. And the ordination and lay ministry of women are new and potentially threatening challenges to the Catholic tradition, challenges which are being pressed ever more vigorously.

Women seek to be ordained precisely when the ranks of male priests are thinned out by retirement, aging, death, and the dearth of fresh vocations. The sacramental ministry of the Catholic Church is being stretched to its limits, and the people are not being fed, at least not in the way to which they were accustomed. It may be that God is not leaving the decision in the hands of the church, no matter how many statements the magisterium issues to the effect that only men can be priests and for whatever more or less plausible reasons from Scripture and symbolism.

The situation resembles more than a little the one found in Acts 6:1–6 (cf. pp. 00–00). There, too, the needs of the people outstripped the capacity of the appointed ministers. There as well, the current model of ministry was highly symbolic: the twelve represented Israel, and their table-service symbolized their spiritual authority. In the face of the challenge posed by God's activity—the growth in numbers, the changing population, the dissension—the apostles were able to distinguish service from symbol. In so doing, they discovered the deeper meaning of their own service, and used the symbol to transfer authority to others. These others, we recall, were chosen by the community which had discerned in them wisdom and the Holy Spirit.

But how can the church today know whether it is right to reverse two thousand years of precedent and ordain women? It *cannot* know, unless it discerns the activity of God in the women of the church today, and that can be made available only by the narrative of that activity by the faithful.

The symbolisms of the past will remain intact without this stimulus. The Scripture will be heard to say the same thing over and over again eternally, unless our hearing is renewed by the story being told us now by the Spirit. Without the narrative of the experience of God, discernment cannot begin, and decisions are theologically counterfeit.

Whose narratives should be heard? Those of men now ordained, to be sure. But also those of women who seek ordination. Without a place to narrate the story of what they consider a call from God, how can the authenticity of that call be discerned by the church? Another narrative can be heard, that spoken by those who have been ministered to by women. What testimony do they give? Was the Word of God preached with integrity and power? Were the sacraments celebrated with reverence and care? Was the gift of prophecy and reconciliation alive in them? Was there a distinctive way of articulating the faith available to women, the loss of which impoverishes the church's faith?

This narrative is available to the Catholic church even now. The churches in which women have been ordained ministers for some time have a narrative of that experience which is available to the Catholic community. But even within the Catholic Church, there is a long and powerful story which demands hearing, the story of generations of ministry carried out by religious women, and those ministered to by them. There are women in the church who *have* evangelized, catechized, prophesied, and healed among the people. What is their narrative? And how has that been discerned by the countless Catholics evangelized, catechized, and healed by them? Did God do "signs and wonders" through them? If this narrative is not being spoken, something is said about the state of the church. If there is not even an interest in its being spoken (because of a conviction there is nothing to hear?), something even stronger is being said.

Divorced and Remarried in the Church

Here is an issue of *fellowship* which is present in other churches (often in the form of implicit ostracism), but is critical in the Catholic Church. It is no overstatement to say that vast numbers of people who wish to be in communion are not because they have divorced and remarried. By canon law, they are excluded from the sacraments so long as they stay in this state. Since the Catholic tradition is rooted in the sacramental life, especially the Eucharist, this effectively means exclusion from the church's life. Annulment procedures have been streamlined, but they are still lengthy and arbitrary.

As a result, many raised in the Catholic tradition join other church bodies, but with varying degrees of uneasy conscience. Others, taking seriously the teaching that the Catholic church is the "only true church," and that joining other communions is apostasy and involves heresy, limit their losses and, with varying degrees of bitterness, leave the visible body of believers altogether. There are local adjustments: sometimes the clergy of a place will "allow" such persons to receive communion. But it is a practice in tension with the overall norm, and no less arbitrary, if more merciful, than annulment procedures. The net effect is that millions of people who wish to be in communion are not, and are in fact excluded from the church's pastoral care.

The studies of Scripture scholars on the sayings of Jesus forbidding marriage have not had much impact on the church's practice, even though they show how even in the early church, the hard saying of Jesus (Mark 10:10-12) was reread in the light of complex religious and social circumstances (cf. Matt. 5:31-32; 19:3-9; 1 Cor. 7:12-16). Just as the church of today, the church of the first generation had to struggle at once with the seriousness of Jesus' demands, and the strictures of complex worldly existence.

The church in every age must respond to the words of Jesus with creative fidelity. This does not mean a rigid or mechanical application, but the creative fidelity which means true obedience, and which translates the words accurately within changed social and religious structures. Is marriage the same reality in twentieth century America as it was in first century Palestine, or even in twentieth century Ghana? In a world which demands that a single couple bear the entire burden of fidelity, while the "other kingdom" insists it is only a burden and not a blessing; in a world whose societal complexity creates stresses on relationships of every kind qualitatively distinct from any known before; in a world where the support of family, friends, or even church is harder and harder to assume; are we still talking about the same phenomenon when we say "marriage"?

Not only our world but also our understanding of what it means to be human has developed. The Christian asserts that it is precisely because of the work of the Spirit of Jesus leading us into new understanding of his words that this change has occurred. Because of this assertion, we need to ask about our reflex understanding of the key word "adultery" in Jesus' saying. I do not question the sinful reality or tragic alienation that is adultery. By no means. I simply ask whether everything we designate by that term is what Jesus meant. In particular we need to ask about the concept "state of adultery." Like that other category, "state of perfection," it is a best a loose and frequently a misleading phrase. Can one be in a state of adultery where there is no relationship being betrayed? The question here, of course, is whether there can still be a marriage without a genuine commitment by both partners. Is it realistic, or honest, to say that a woman who was regularly beaten together with her children by her husband, and then left him and divorced so that he would have no claim on her or the children, then met a man who could be her husband and her children's father, is committing adultery? Or that the man who marries such a woman commits adultery? We might, but I think Jesus would not. The issue raised is whether the Catholic church will continue to decide in this matter on the basis of law, or on the basis of the Spirit, which requires discernment.

How can the church begin this discernment? A starting point is the recognition that God is not absent from the lives of those who, for whatever reason, find themselves alienated from the visible church. Not only does God act in their lives, but they have a narrative of experience important for the church to hear. What have these excommunicated Catholics actually experienced? Was their divorce a matter of convenience or a question of salvation? Do they see God at work even in this breakup, and why? Was their remarriage an act of cynical selfishness or a move toward spiritual health? Are their lives driven by lust or care? These questions cannot be answered by canon law or Scripture. They are not available for sociological analysis or statistical breakdown. They can begin to be answered only by those who are now outside communion but whose faith in God is alive and genuine, and who, somewhat like Cornelius, await the Lord in prayer. If the church does not care to hear these stories then it cares not for the Word of God, for the Word is spoken there as well.

Homosexuality in the Church

This is an issue of fellowship faced by all churches today. It is made more difficult by the tension generated by feelings of threat and rejection on every side, and by the postures of miltancy and defensiveness adopted by many. On one side, we find the bald citation of New Testament passages condemning homosexuality, without sensitivity either to the formal nature of those passages (e.g., Rom. 1:26–27; 1 Cor. 6:9–11), or the fact that the lists in question contain other categories within which many heterosexuals fall. On the other side, strident claims to a right of recognition by the church are sometimes made precisely on the *basis* of being homosexual. Increasingly, the poles separate, with "gay" and "straight" churches existing side by side but not together. This is a situation in which the very nature of the church is threatened. If the church is to be a community in which there is neither Jew nor Greek, male nor female, slave nor free (cf. Gal. 3:28), in which all people are to form one new humanity established in Christ (Eph. 2:14–17), then it is tragic and distorting to have a church in which persons are excluded from communion simply on the basis of sexual orientation—no matter what their behavior or attitude. It is equally tragic and distorting to have other "churches" whose sole badge of membership is proclaiming a particular sexual orientation. Both become sectarian, and in a way not much different from the Jew/Greek distinction. In that case, too, it did not matter whether one was a sinful Jew or a devout Gentile. Ethnic status alone mattered. So here also, gender or sexual orientation as the only basis for inclusion or exclusion leads to the twisting of the church's nature and vocation.

It would be wrong-headed to deny the complexity or difficulty of this issue. It is certainly one about which I know too little. But I have listened to enough stories to make me question my presuppositions about where God *cannot* be at work. That homosexual activity can be sinful, I have no doubt, any more than I doubt that heterosexual activity can be sinful. That a style of life built upon sexual promiscuity and pleasure, while claiming to be Christian, is self-contradictory, I am certain—whether it is gay or straight in orientation. But I am not certain how central and determinative one's sexual activity is before God. Nor am I sure how limited God is in the ability to give grace and evoke faith.

I have been forced to wonder, for example, at the way committed, sincere, and intelligent believers have discovered that their lifelong struggle against a homosexual orientation has been in effect a rejection of the way God has created them. For some of these men and women, the acceptance of this "fact" about themselves has been the *beginning* of a genuine search for God's will in their lives. In the disciplined, by no means self-indulgent spiritual journals of some of my students, I have read how the acknowledgment of their sexual identity has been tantamount to a conversion experience. I report this, though I have not digested it myself.

How can we begin to exercise discernment in the church on this question, without the narratives of both gay and straight believers? Is it proper to equate a homosexual orientation with sexual immorality, any more than it is to equate alcoholism with drunkenness? For that matter, is sexual immorality itself, of whatever sort, grounds for exclusion from the church? Are we in a situation analogous to that of the incestuous man in Corinth, or the Ethiopian eunuch on the road to Gaza? Is faith in God and the obedience of faith not available to gay people? I do not like to think about these things, for they call my presuppositions into question. That is why we need the narratives of those involved. And if we discover, when we hear these narratives, that ''they have received the same gift as us,'' what will our response be? Will the church, like Peter, say, ''Who are we to withstand God?'' Or, will it deserve his rebuke, ''Why are you testing God?''

Narrative and Discernment

It may be thought, from the way I have cast the cases above, that I think the church's discernment and decision can only go one way, and that is to say ''yes.'' But that is emphatically what I do *not* think. That would make discernment meaningless. The church must, if it is to test every spirit, sometimes say ''no,'' for not every spirit is of God (cf. 1 John 4:1-6). If this is the case for every spirit, it is all the more so with every narrative. Not every story narrated to the church is a story of God's work. Some stories reveal the work of idolatry and sin. For this very reason, it is important that the church hear the narratives. The case of incest in 1 Corinthians 5 showed us a deviance the church could not tolerate and still remain church. The situation of Matthew 18 showed us how an open defiance of the church's authority to correct demanded the rebel's exclusion. We also saw how open opposition in the Acts 15 narrative served the cause of discernment. My point is not that the church can only decide one way, but for the church to reach decision as a community articulating its faith in God, it requires these narratives for discernment.

It is all the more necessary, then, to have some clarity about a ''narrative of experience'' in the church, if it is to play such a critical role in the discernment process. Both the term ''narrative'' and ''experience'' require some qualification.

I use the word narrative here to mean the ordered expression of personal memory. It is not a collection of anecdotes, or a set of opinions, informed or not, on particular subjects. Still less is it the "making of a case," or a kind of polemical pleading. The issue before the church's discernment is not "my rights," but God's will. The decision of the church should not be based on the most powerful pressure group or advocacy, but on the activity of God in the world. This can be offered the church by the ordered expression of personal memory. Because it is a story, it is available to others more immediately than other forms of speech. Because it is "my story" or "our story," it involves risk and a certain unavoidable vulnerability. The narrative of experience is a form of witnessing. As all witnessing, it is personal, but not self-preoccupied. One speaks of what one knows, while recognizing that this firsthand knowledge is always partial and interested. Such recital requires sufficient detachment and discipline to order the testimony. The narrative of experience is not a formless exercise in self-expression, but a structured account of personal religious experience.

If the term "narrative" gets at the form of the speech, the term "experience" gets us to the subject matter, and it is harder to describe. Clearly, not every kind of "experience" is appropriate for recitation in the assembly. Yet defining what is fitting is difficult. Two extremes can be eliminated. On the one hand, the undigested stuff of daily life does not constitute experience for the church's discernment. At the other extreme, peak religious experiences, those encounters with the "Holy" which call us into question, are certainly pertinent, but alone are not enough. What is needed is the way such religious experiences and daily life come together; the way what we perceive as all powerful and transcendent gives structure to the rest of our lives: how it actually has given shape to our past and present. The intrusion of power creates patterns in our life. The point of our narrative should be the power. But we need enough of the pattern to locate it. A narrative expressing such experience is not a form of exhibitionism but a form of praise, showing forth God's revelation in our lives.

But here exactly is where discernment is most necessary. The meaning, adequacy, and implications of personal religious experience and history call forth the community's discernment as it seeks to decipher God's Word to it in the present moment. Not every spirit is the Holy Spirit, not every word God's Word. Not every "turning" is a conversion. Not every kingdom is the kingdom of God. There are "religious experiences" which are not encounters with the true God. We can, as individuals, mistake the movements of the Spirit. We may be deluded, and either consciously or not distort both our experience and the narrative of it, shaping them to our desire. We may think we are being moved by the Spirit of God, but may actually be enslaved by idolatry and sin. That is why the *narrative* is critical, for it includes the results as well as the causes, the patterns as well as the powers, and therefore enables others to discern whether this is the way the Spirit of God works in human lives.

The warning against false prophets in Matt.7:15–20 twice repeats "You will know them by their fruits," and we can apply this to the patterns created in our lives by the powers by which we live. Paul has listed the fruits of the Holy Spirit's direction: "Love, joy, peace, patience, kindness, goodness, faithfulness, gentleness, self-control" (Gal. 5:22–23). And he lists the "works of the flesh" which militate against the Spirit: "Fornication, impurity, licentiousness, idolatry, sorcery, enmity, strife, jealousy, anger, selfishness, dissension, party spirit, envy, drunkenness, carousing, and the like" (Gal. 5:19–21). The Spirit of God, when truly at work, leaves traces in our story. The church does have a way to discern the Spirit's work, but only if the fruits are made available by narrative.

Such a process of discernment is obviously hazardous and therefore requires great delicacy. Most of us would prefer norms more steady and machinery less personal for our decision-making process. But the need for spiritual discernment in the process of reaching decision is derived from the very essence of the church's life. When by-laws and customs, or codes and unreflected Scripture citations, replace the testing of the Spirit in the church, then the church may reveal itself in the process of reaching decision, but it won't be as a community of faith in the Spirit.

For the process to work at all, certain qualities are clearly required both of those who speak and those who hear. On the part of all, a conscious commitment to the presence of the Spirit in the assembly is necessary. The context in which speaking and listening is done can be one of reverential silence before the mystery, once this commitment to the name of Jesus is genuinely and explicitly made. The community does not seek the display of rhetoric or the flash of personality, but the Word of the Lord. In an atmosphere of silence and awe, there is less temptation to turn narrative into polemic and discernment into judgment. The community listens and speaks before the gaze of one who "knowest the hearts of all" (Acts 1:24).

On the part of those who speak, there should be modesty before the mystery, a simplicity which allows the story to unfold without self-aggrandizement, either in the direction of self-glory or self-castigation. God is the subject of the discourse. At the same time, the human texture of experience must be allowed to emerge. The mechanical repetition of platitudes like "the Lord said to me" is useless. It begs the question, first of all. What the community needs to do is discern whether it *was* the Lord who "said to you," and in what way. The speaker helps the community by letting it see the worldly circumstances of religious experience. This requires of the speaker an attention to real life and how one's response to the Holy has formed patterns of faith and idolatry.

On the part of those who listen, there is need for as much self-discernment and self-criticism as discernment of the other's story. I need to question my presuppositions about God's limits. To be open to new ways of hearing God's Word I must be critical of the ways my previous hearing has become closed and exclusive. Perhaps God is not speaking to me in the story of the other; but I will never know if I do not allow the possibility that God *may* be speaking. The listener must attend to the story being told, and the story already known by the community, testing for what is new and what is familiar. The listener wants to be open to the new, but is insistent on signs of continuity. If the story rings false, contradicts absolutely the story already told, discernment demands the open and honest expression of objection and opposition. If the voice of opposition is silent, discernment may not have taken place. Tacit approval of every voice, through fear of confrontation, will make the church lose its identity as quickly and surely as the rejection of every voice, through fear of change.

In practical terms, there are capacities of speaking and hearing which are as important as these attitudes. Perhaps the spirit of discernment is alive in a church, but cannot be exercised for lack of words to tell the story, and lack of a framework for the hearing of it. Theology must attend to people's ability to tell their story as well as to hear it. How can this be done? To that question we now turn.

5

DEVICES

Even essays for idealists must eventually get down to cases. No good is done by criticizing present ways of reaching decision unless at least the sketch of an alternative be presented. In this chapter, I want to suggest some ways in which the decision-making process might be encouraged in the local church. The local church has been the focus throughout this book. As it is the best place to think about the nature of the church, so is it the best place to begin to shape a theologically informed way of reaching decision. If the process is not in place at the local level, it will not be at the ecumenical level. Decisions made at the higher levels of church organizations will remain remote from the church's life, unless those decisions have first been generated by the discernment of communities at the local level.

What I am suggesting here is a way of doing pastoral theology in an active and constructive sense. The person who helps the local church learn how to articulate its faith when it goes about making decision is also helping to bring the church into being in the first place, helping the church to become itself. The task is a large one, and the implications are great. Starting to work at this means beginning to move in a direction which has not been heavily traveled for some time. Not only are there not many markers on the way, but the goal itself is still only ill-defined. In this, it is like the response of faith.

A good first step is the recognition of the difficulties. Some of these are tactical and some conceptual. Tactical problems are those of procedure: how do we move from one way of doing things to another? The everyday but hard realities of physical bodies and space must be considered here: schedules, room space, lighting, furniture arrangement, numbers, and the like. These are not unimportant considerations. It is not easy to practice, or learn to practice, ''discernment of the Spirit'' in an auditorium filled with people and wired for sound. A living room or small chapel does better. People sitting in a circle can speak to each other and listen better than if they are all facing a podium. Testing the Spirit of God is more pleasant in an atmosphere of leisure than one of haste and tension.

In light of these factors, it is best to begin to learn this way of doing things by forming small groups, and then building slowly to the level of the congregation as a whole. We are convinced that where ''two or three are gathered'' in the name of Jesus, there is a realization of the church. We seek, after all, not a different system of governance, but a new style of interaction within the community which will foster discernment in decision making. To learn to do this, there must be an atmosphere of trust, but also the practical opportunity for active participation: practice, repetition, and response between the members. This learning of theology is not first a theoretical enterprise, but a practical one, as practical as learning to speak a language.

Having such small groups within the congregation will pose at least two other problems. The temptation to constitute groups on the basis of congeniality or like-mindedness must be avoided. Even in its smallest embodiment, the church should be a place where differences can be reconciled. In addition, when it is time to move the process to a larger level of the assembly, members of small groups will need to resist the urge to stay within the security of the smaller assembly, where they could speak more freely and be heard more generously.

The biggest practical problem, however, is the perception that there are too many meetings going on in the local church already than anyone can possibly attend. There will be an obvious and understandable resistance to forming other groups if they are seen as ''just another meeting.'' A clear understanding of the nature of this group and of its importance for the life of the community must be in place from the start. For this reason, the function of this sort of group must be distinguished from those already in place.

Not only are there many other meetings, but they tend to systematically separate precisely the elements which need to be brought together, if decision making is to become a theologically responsible process, an articulation of the church's faith. Vestry meetings and their equivalents are the places where the real ''decisions'' are made in many churches. There, the elected or *ex officio* leaders of the assembly debate and decide the hard issues of finance and personnel; position papers and dossiers and financial reports receive ardent attention. But this business is, well, business. There is little place here for the narrative of experience, or the citation of Scripture, except in the anecdotal and tangential way that makes these meetings long.

Life narratives are now told in contexts where decisions—except the most individual and internal—are not made. Personal stories are told in individual or group pastoral counseling sessions, or in support groups sponsored by the church. These narratives, however, rarely focus on the specifically religious dimensions of the narrator's life, and even less frequently are used to interpret the Scripture.

Finally, many churches have meetings for the study of the Bible, whether in Sunday school, adult education, or smaller study groups. The emphasis in such groups is usually on the "study" of the text, as guided by contemporary biblical scholarship. This is frequently carried out at a rather sophisticated level, but the element of personal faith narrative is not often found in this context. And there is even less connection with the making of decisions which affect the life of the whole community.

In effect, then, local congregations often have all the components for theological decision making already in the life of the church, but they are kept in separate places. This separation narrows and makes less powerful each of the elements. They need to be brought together in a single place and fused into a single process, the catalyst for which is community discernment.

It would be unrealistic and destructive to replace the present structures of the church with some more "spiritual" assembly. There are at least three reasons. First, each kind of meeting has its own legitimate function: there is a place for financial analysis, pastoral counseling, and Bible study in the church. None of these should be abandoned. Second, decisions must continue to be made within the present structure, simply for the community's survival. The world will not go away until we can develop a theologically more sensitive approach to decision making. Third, any move toward a "charismatic" structure would result in chaos unless people were prepared, by having learned to practice (and it is a gift which requires practice) discernment. The church would quickly find itself in the same confusion as the Corinthian congregation. The beginning must be made from below, not from above; it must begin with life, not with order.

The proper beginning, then, can be made in small groups which gather in the name of Jesus for precisely one purpose: to do theology. The groups must be small enough for face-to-face interaction; large enough to ensure continuance; diverse enough to enable the expression of different viewpoints. The aim is to generate the capacity to think theologically; to detect the experience of God in the context of wordly life; to "narrate" that experience; to discern the movement of the Spirit it reveals; to interpret the Scripture in the light of the manifold narratives of the group; to decide for God. The more this sort of thing is done within the small groups, the more this way of thinking and speaking will characterize the other activities of the church. This is desirable, for it is not the special academic interest of a group which is being cultivated, but the life of the entire church which seeks articulation.

Once such groups begin, however, they face other difficulties more conceptual than tactical. Most people in the church do not know *how* to tell their story as one of faith experience; do not know *how* to read the Scripture as pertinent to life; do not even know the meaning of discernment; regard silence as a threatening, not a creative, ambience. The first task of a group, in fact, can be the candid acknowledgment of these difficulties. They are shared by all of us, for this has not been our way in the church. Few are experts in this process. Those who are have as much to learn as those who are not, for their expertise consists only in this, their desire that the process should begin and the church live as a community of faith. The first story told by us as a group may be the story of how we are incapable of doing this thing we have set ourselves to doing. As each one tells this tale, it moves from the level of a personal inadequacy to a church need. In this way, the moats of fear between us begin to be bridged. This is a beginning. But greater difficulties remain.

We want to learn to speak of God and God's activity in the world in a way that respects the Mystery, and that also recognizes the complexity of real human life. We wish to develop the capacity to speak God's praises without falling into mechanical and artificial piety. This kind of speech is hard to come by. As different meetings have divided up the segments of the theological decision process, so the linguistic capacities of most believers dwell in separate compartments.

Language which is recognizably "theological" is also, in the minds of many, certifiably dull. Terms like "faith" and "grace" and "sin" have been petrified by generations of pious usage, and are rarely seen to connect to such mundane things as my daily schedule or nightly lovemaking. To ask someone, then, to speak of "an experience of grace" is to ask something literally impossible. The belief about the reality of grace has no correspondence in everyday life, but is part of a closed system of symbols. The reality of grace is not easily correlated with the time we fell in love, when I first knew that you knew me utterly as I was and not as I wished to be known and accepted me anyway that way, and how frightening and freeing an experience that was.

The language of Scripture is equally inaccessible to life. When I hear Paul speak of "the grace of God," it may leave a warm sensation, but it does not enter the same brain that figures percentages on loans, or analyzes cell structures. And if the words do enter there, I engage in the intellectual game of distancing: "What did Paul mean by grace, anyway?" In either case, I find it hard to connect his words to the depression I feel at not finding work. Not even Bible study, which tells me all I want to know about the Corinthian congregation and the Pauline journeys, helps me see how "the grace of God" has much to do with us sitting in this room together because we are supposed to be thinking theologically.

Another splinter of our language is used to express our life experience. This language is equidistant from that of theology and Bible. When we use the language of "self-revelation," we use a mixture of everyday language and the clichés of sociology and phychology—"psychobabble." We tell our tales facilely as stories of traumas and conflicts, complexes and stages, obsessions and compulsions, self-realizations and self-actualizations. We think this talk simply corresponds to "facts." We are not able or willing to see that this language, too, is conventional and increasingly rigid, and even at best only a formal and partial categorizing of our life. Many of us would not think to tell this same story as one of original sin and idolatry, of conversion and faith.

And if there are such watertight compartments in our language, we can be sure that there are also such compartments in our minds and hearts, so that the language about God, the language of the Bible and the language about ourselves remain sealed off from each other. It comes as a shock when I confidently discourse about my recent nervous breakdown and a friend asks, "Do you think God might be calling you to some sort of conversion in this chaos?" It does not compute. The worlds do not touch.

These separate symbolic worlds *can* come together, but only by forc-
ing them to, and the doing of it is a messy business. That is why groups
should have no other task but to learn these capacities. The scholarly study
of theology, the academic study of the Bible, and the theoretical analysis
of the person will only keep the realms of language separate and increasingly distant. Only in the give and take of people committed to the task
of learning the language of living faith will the merger be effected.

In the *attempt* to speak of God with a language which touches ground,
and speak of ourselves with a language which reaches beyond us, and to
learn of both from the language of the Bible, the element of discernment
also comes into play. As I try to describe an experience of transforming
power I can attribute only to God, those who listen can ask for clarification, can doubt and wonder, can test my words against their own. And as
I listen to them, I learn as well to test my story, and discover the deeper
resonances of our shared narrative. As children learn the range and nuance
of language not alone by hearing but above all by speaking, so do we all
with the language of the faith in the church. Theologians and Scripture
scholars help us as grammarians and librarians, but they cannot define the
language of faith beforehand. Indeed, they need to learn a new task as well,
that of listening to as many stories as they can.

The learning of the language of faith, however, need not be altogether
haphazard. The practical steps can be taken to develop a living theological
vocabulary. Both intend not to coin new words, but to revivify and enrich
old ones. The first step is the vigorous use of the insights given by the
analysis of religious experience.

The religious experiences and convictions of countless peoples, together
with their myths and practices, have been carefully described and rigor-
ously analyzed by disciplined observers, whose findings are available in
convenient texts. In them, one can find certain consistent components of
the life before God beneath an astonishing variety of expressions. One consistent element, for example, is the way religious experiences are ones of
a power which intrudes into everyday life. This power has the ability to
organize time and space around itself. Looking at the structure of sacred
times and places, therefore, gives us some clues as to the kind of power
they point to, and where it appeared. Now, it is possible to shift this kind
of observation from those texts to our lives. We can look at the patterns
of our lives with new eyes, and wonder about the power which gives them

structure. My avoidance of certain places, and my obsessive observance of certain times may have a deeper religious significance than at first appears. They may help me see what is truly powerful in my eyes, that by which I measure my worth and around which I structure my days. The categories of religious experience, in other words, can become diagnostic categories for the understanding of our everyday life. This does not happen automatically or even easily, for real life is resistant to such perceptions. Learning to look at life for its significant patterns requires discipline. But it is possible, and it is a beginning.

The language of religious experience is not a panacea, for it can become as abstract as that of classical theological language, if separated from the experiences it seeks to describe. But if those using it practice discernment— testing, questioning, supporting each other in the venture—this language can begin to crack the walls between theology and life.

And if the awareness of how power draws life around itself helps me detect the patterns of my own existence, it can also help me read the language of the Scripture with new eyes. Why? Because it is precisely to the reality of religious existence which the symbols and stories of the Bible most directly speak. How humans exist before God in the world is the subject of the sacred texts, and they speak as pertinently to our religious experience as to those of our forebears. The stories of the burning bush (Exod. 3:1-6), of the call of Isaiah (Isa. 6:1-13) and of the Gerasene demoniac (Mark 5:1-20) not only grow more vivid when viewed this way, but look increasingly like the stories we tell each other. So the reading of our lives brings the Bible alive, and the reading of the Bible helps us decipher the Word being spoken in our lives. Paul's attack on idolatry in Rom. 1:18-32 not only rings true as a description of religious experience, but has frightening power to illuminate and convict my own patterns of clinging and self-deception. The language of religious experience, therefore, can help bridge the now separate worlds of ordinary life, the Bible, and theological concepts. As the two parts of the story of revelation become mutually more reinforcing, less external mediation will be necessary.

Another practical procedure, one already used in many churches, is to begin with the narrative texts of the Scripture themselves as the stimulus and model for the narrative of faith. From the way these narratives speak of God, so can we learn. And as these witnesses never lose the direct touch of the human, so, we hope, will our language about God remain in touch with the contours of our days. Talk about God should not diminish but transfigure the language about God's creation. A group which came together on a regular basis, placed itself in silence, read a narrative passage together, then began, one by one, to narrate their diverse appropriations of that passage in their lives, that group would begin to learn the language of faith.

Many are the texts appropriate for this process: the parables of Jesus are used by many people with great effectiveness. Equally powerful are the narratives of the Old Testament, such as those telling of the rise and fall of Saul, or the family of David. An almost perfect passage for this purpose is the one which has dominated this particular book, namely Acts 10–15, the story of the conversion of Cornelius and the Apostolic Council. If the story is read section by section, it can evoke precisely the sort of questions which will generate theological reflection. After coming together in the prayer of silence, for example, let us suppose a member of the group reads of the vision of Cornelius and that of Simon. The first thing that would happen in the group's perception of itself as a community gathered to hear the words which God has commanded would be reinforced (cf. Acts 10:33).

But the passage also leads naturally to questions about our individual and communal lives. Do we have experiences like these visions? Is our sense of God's presence in prayer as vivid as Cornelius's? Or, are we confused and perplexed like Peter? Do we discover that the narrative of others' experiences helps clarify our own, as Peter found in the story of Cornelius a clarification of his own story?

These questions can be followed by others which are more challenging, but equally necessary for discernment. How can we say that an experience is from God? How did Peter know? Or did he ever know, with certainty? Is it a part of faith that when you decide for God, you cannot be sure you have? As the story of Acts moves deeper into conflict and decision making, even more provocative questions will be asked of the group, and in the process of answering them, it will discover itself becoming church.

The narrative of Acts 10–15 not only gives us a picture of the church reaching decision as a theological process, but also gives us a model of what role theology can play in the life of the church. More than that the narrative of Acts 10–15, when read by the church in faith and discernment, can become the vehicle for doing theology for and in the church. This text can effect that which it describes.

Bibliographical Note

Among many works in which religious experience is described, certain ones are classic. Rudolf Otto, *The Idea of the Holy*, Eng. trans. J. Harvey (New York and London: Oxford University Press, 1958) lacks precision just where one would want it, but the fundamental framework it provides is invaluable. The same can be said of virtually any of Mircea Eliade's many works, of which the most useful might be *The Sacred and the Profane, The Nature of Religion*, Eng. trans. W. Trask (New York: Harcourt, Brace and World, 1959). Gerardus van der Leeuw, *Religion in Essence and Manifestation* 2 vols., Eng. trans. J. E. Turner (New York: Harper & Row, Harper Torchbooks, 1963) is drier, but is very fine in its consistent attention to the factor of power in religious experience. Joachim Wach, *The Comparative Study of Religions*, (New York: Columbia University Press, 1958) has a splendid first chapter devoted to authentic religious experience. Two works which help locate religious experience within societal functions are Bronislaw Malinowski's *Magic, Science and Religion, and Other Essays*, (Garden City, N.Y.: Doubleday & Co., Anchor Books, 1954), and Peter Berger's *The Sacred Canopy* (Garden City, N.Y.: Doubleday & Co., Anchor Books, 1967).